St. James Parish Library
Marietta, Georgia

THE CHURCH SUPPER

New Trends in Cooking for Crowds

OTHER BOOKS BY THE AUTHOR

Cooking for Crowds Bethany Press, October 1963
The Saga of Texas Cookery Encino Press, October 1973
BREAD Encino Press, December 1975

THE CHURCH SUPPER

New Trends in Cooking for Crowds

by Sarah Morgan

THE BETHANY PRESS
Saint Louis   Missouri

© 1976 by The Bethany Press

All rights reserved. No part of this book may be reproduced by any method without the publisher's written permission. Address The Bethany Press, Box 179, St. Louis, Mo. 63166.

Library of Congress Cataloging in Publication Data

Morgan, Sarah.
  The church supper.

  1. Cookery for institutions, etc. I. Title.
TX820.M618   641.5'7   76-8468
ISBN 0-8272-0437-X
ISBN 0-8272-0438-8 pbk.

Cover art by DeVere Shoop

Manufactured in the United States of America

FOREWORD

The custom of serving church suppers has been in existence for many, many years and no doubt will continue to be for many years to come, probably as long as the organized church exists. Eating together is one of the real joys of Christian fellowship. Jesus recognized man's need for food to satisfy physical hunger and gave his eternal blessing to the fellowship of eating together by his miracles of feeding the multitude.

Since food is an essential part of man's life, I believe it should be treated as a sacred part of his existence. It should be prepared and consumed with dignity and gratefulness because nothing reflects man's life more than what he eats, the way he prepares it, and how he serves it.

Someone has said "the history of every nation lies visible on its table." It can also be said that the history of any given group's heritage can be gauged by its eating habits, the preparation and serving of its foods. In fact, the careful preparation and serving of good food, whether in the fellowship hall of the church or in the home, are not only an expression of one of the finer arts but also one of the joys of civilized living.

This book is written, researched, collected, and tested for the express purpose of helping those men and women in the church who volunteer or are drafted to plan and prepare the church suppers, or for that matter, any meal serving a crowd. It has been my observation that not many of these people have had formal training or experience in quantity cooking. And for those who are trained or experienced in quantity cooking, I hope they will find here some new and exciting ideas to make their sometime tiresome task easier and more pleasant.

The recipes in this book, with a few exceptions, are for fifty or multiples of fifty. A crowd is never just twenty-five, fifty, or one hundred, and so on, but I have found this measuring standard to work well when cooking in quantities.

It is my sincere hope that in this book will be found sufficient information and concrete help for all those who work to make the church fellowship of eating together occasions of real joy and a lasting blessing for everyone.

Sarah Morgan,
Fort Worth, Texas

CONTENTS

PART I

PRELIMINARIES TO QUANTITY COOKING

Planning Ahead	13
Keeping Kitchen Records	14
The Search for Cooking Talent	16
Equipment, Appliances, and Utensils	17
Measures and Equivalents	18
Metric Conversion Factors	19
A Guide to Purchasing Food for Fifty	21
A General Guide For Amounts of Prepared Foods	24
A Guide for Average Individual Servings	25
Seasonings for Quantity Cooking	27
Herbs and Spices	27
Leavening Agents	29
Thickening Agents	29
Oven Temperatures for Baking and Roasting	29
Making Use of Convenience Foods in Quantity Cooking	30
Serving the Crowd	31
Tastes and Prejudices	31

PART II

POTLUCK SUPPERS
The Potluck Supper 35
An Authentic Potluck 35
The Planned Potluck 36
The Supplemented Potluck 37

PART III

TRADITIONAL AND NEW RECIPES
Appetizers 41
Beverages 42
    Coffee 42
    Tea 46
    Chocolate Drinks 47
    Punches 49
Bread 55
    Yeast Breads 55
    Directions for Freezing 67
    Yeast Bread Rolls 68
    Suggestions for Shapes and Sizes 68
    Sweet Yeast Rolls 72
        Fillings for Sweet Rolls 74
    Quick Breads 76
      Biscuits 76
      Muffins 78
      Corn Breads 79
    Sweet Breads 82
    Creole Doughnuts 85
    A Pizza for a Party 86
    Cream Puffs 88
    Cheese Balls 89
    Cheese Wafers 89
Soups 91
Relishes and Garnishes 99

Salads
- Fruit Salads ... 102
  - Dressings ... 103
- Vegetable-Fruit Combinations ... 106
- Vegetable Salads ... 108
- Cabbage Salads ... 110
- Potato Salads ... 112
- Chicken, Shrimp, and Tuna Salads ... 114
- Congealed Salads ... 117

Salad Dressings ... 120
- French ... 121
- Mayonnaise ... 122
- Cooked Salad Dressing ... 124

Sauces for Meats and Vegetables ... 126

Sandwiches ... 134
- General Information ... 134
- Hamburger ... 136
- Other Popular Sandwiches ... 137

Meats ... 140
- Beef ... 140
- Pork ... 152
- Lamb ... 157
- Chicken ... 158
- Turkey ... 164
- Fish ... 166

Vegetables ... 169
- Pasta and Starchy Vegetables ... 181

Desserts ... 186
- General Information ... 186
- Pie Crusts ... 187
- Crumb Crusts ... 188
- Shells ... 190

Crust for Cobblers	191
Pies	192
Cobblers	196
Cakes	203
Cookies	204
Puddings	205
Frostings and Icings	209
Fillings and Sweet Sauces	211
Custards	213

PART IV
CASEROLES
Tasty Casseroles	219

PART V
A SHORT CULINARY TRAVELOGUE
Eating with Some Other Countries

Denmark	231
France	233
Germany	234
Hungary	236
Italy	238
Mexico	240
Spain	241
Sweden	243

PART I

PRELIMINARIES TO QUANTITY COOKING

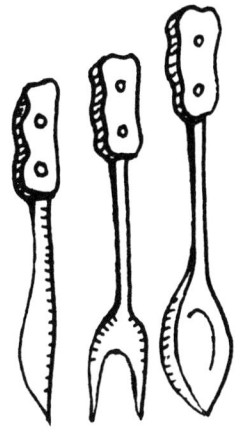

PRELIMINARIES

PLANNING AHEAD

Cooking for large crowds, whether for church suppers or for any other quantity cooking, needs well-formulated and detailed plans made in advance, and *put in writing,* to make the task a work of love and joy and not a chore. A well-organized group working for the good of all concerned and with a spirit of joyous adventure can be an everlasting blessing no matter how arduous the task.

The group or organization responsible for preparing and planning the meals should sit down together and make definite arrangements for specific menus, with specific persons appointed to perform specific duties. The records of this meeting should be put in writing and kept in the kitchen. The cost of the preparations and the possible income from the meals should be given definite consideration and should also become a part of the records. Included with all of these plans should be the plans for *supervised* serving of the meals.

One of the big disappointments for the cooks who have labored, planned, and executed an excellent meal is to have it served in such a careless manner that it loses its importance. I have found that if the name of the person or persons responsible for supervising the serving is not only placed in the records, but also posted on the kitchen or dining room door, the meal will be served in good taste and in an orderly fashion.

Keeping kitchen records. Through the years that I have helped, supervised, or worked with cooking for crowds, the one thing that I have decided can definitely improve morale, avoid hurt feelings, and lighten the work load of the workers is a record, *kept in the kitchen,* not in the church library or in the church office. This record should give the names of the workers, the dates, and the menus, and other details which may otherwise be forgotten. I am giving here a short form—as a suggestion—that might be printed and kept, after it is filled out, for easy record keeping.

To be filled out and filed in the kitchen records
CHURCH SUPPERS—or other meals served in the church

Date_____ Hour_____

Name of group to be served _____

Name of person making arrangements __ _____

Telephone number _____

Type of meal_____
        full meal   light meal   refreshments

Menu_____

_____

Where served_____
        dining room (fellowship hall) activity room parlor, etc.

Estimated number of plates_____

Price per plate_____

Name of organization or group accepting the responsibility for the serv-

ing _____

                (Signed)_____
                          Name of person representing the organization that accepts the assignment

Results of meal:

Plates served_____

Price received_____

Names of those who worked in preparing, planning, and serving the meal:

_____   _____   _____

_____   _____   _____

Date:_____   (Signed)_____
                                Name of person reporting

The search for cooking talent. We make much of the music, teaching, playing of instruments, preaching, and other talents found in the church or out of the church, but we often forget the one creative talent important to our everyday existence—the preparation of food. Cooking, be it good, bad, or mediocre, we often accept as normal or take for granted. The job of creative and imaginative cooking is one of the noblest of the creative arts and it should be recognized as such wherever it is found. This talent is especially important in quantity cooking since this skill requires more time, energy, and thought than some of the lesser cooking tasks.

The search for cooking talent can be augmented by asking church members, or members of any group, to fill out a form giving their likes, dislikes, their abilities, their experiences, their knowledge, and their desires for helping with quantity cooking assignments. This form is given only as a suggestion, but any group can prepare its own to hand out to all those who are interested in contributing their time and energy to the task. A cross-reference of this information should be made and kept up-to-date. This, too, should be filed with the kitchen records. The information obtained in such a search can mean the difference between a meal-as-usual and one that is long remembered.

A SEARCH FOR COOKING TALENT for church suppers, or other quantity cooking

Name _____
Address _____ Telephone_____
I like to cook _____ yes_____ no_____ sorta'_____
My speciality is _____
I do not have a specialty, but I prefer to cook the following foods:
_____
I have not had experience in quantity cooking, but I am willing to learn_____
I have had experience in quantity cooking
yes_____ no_____
Remarks _____
The following days, time, etc., suit my schedule best for helping with quantity cooking: _____
_____
Remarks: _____

              (Signed)_____

EQUIPMENT, APPLIANCES, AND UTENSILS

Along with other plans for quantity cooking, special consideration should be given to the equipment available. Fortunate, indeed, is the church that has sufficient equipment, supplies, and utensils to do whatever cooking is required. But for those who do not, and there are many, I am giving a list of some basic equipment that may be of help in purchasing what is needed. Since each church and each kitchen will have varying needs, it is impossible here to do any more than make some suggestions which might serve as a check list. Do make an inventory of what you now have and file that list, dated and signed, and place in the kitchen records. Such an inventory should be kept up-to-date.

Equipment list. Basic equipment: stoves, ovens, sinks, refrigerators, freezers, tables, work space, cabinets, cutting boards, built-ins, and perhaps a deep-fry and grills should be a part of the permanent building.

Utensils list. Scales, showing ounces and pounds up to 25 pounds; large pots, six quarts to two-gallon size; large skillets with handles and lids; large saucepans with handles; measuring cups and spoons of varying sizes, beginning with 2-cup to 2-quart size; mixing bowls, 3 or 4 sizes, one about 2-gallon capacity for bread rising; baking dishes for serving casseroles, average size 4 quarts; water pans to hold large kettles when cooking over hot water; wooden spoons, stirring spoons, and serving spoons; whips for beating; ladles; strainers—large, medium, and small; a colander for straining; an electric mixer and a portable electric mixer; baking pans—three or four 20 X 12 X 2-inches; loaf pans for baking bread; an assortment of knives for paring, slicing, etc; spatulas.

There will be other needs and many of those mentioned may not be needed. That is why I suggest you use this as a checklist and make your own.

MEASURES AND EQUIVALENTS

A few of the most commonly used in quantity cooking

2 cups granulated sugar	1 pound
2 1/4 cups brown sugar	1 pound
3 1/3 cups confectioners sugar	1 pound
4 cups flour	1 pound
2 cups butter	1 pound
2 cups rice	1 pound
2 cups cornmeal	10 ounces
2 cups bread crumbs, soft	8 ounces
2 cups chopped or ground beef	1 pound
2 cups ham, ground	1 pound
3 cups chicken, cooked & cubed	1 pound
1 ounce granulated gelatin	4 tablespoons
6 to 8 cups lettuce, shredded	1 pound
2 cups mayonnaise	1 pound

Other Equivalents

2 tablespoons butter	1 ounce
2 tablespoons	1 fluid ounce
3 teaspoons	1 tablespoon
4 tablespoons	1/4 cup
16 tablespoons	1 cup
2 cups	1 pint
2 pints	1 quart
4 quarts	1 gallon

All measures are approximate

The following Metric Conversion Factors are from the U.S. Department of Commerce, National Bureau of Standards, Washington, D.C.

METRIC CONVERSION FACTORS

Approximate Conversions To Metric Measures

Symbol	When you know	Multiply by	To find	Symbol
Mass (Weight)				
oz.	ounces	28	grams	g
lb.	pounds	0.45	kilograms	kg
Volume				
tsp.	teaspoons	5	milliliters	ml
tbsp.	tablespoons	15	milliliters	ml
fl. oz.	fluid ounces	30	milliliters	ml
c.	cups	0.24	liters	l
pt.	pints	0.47	liters	l
qt.	quarts	0.95	liters	l
gal.	gallons	3.8	liters	l
Temperature				
°F	Fahrenheit	5/9 (after subtracting 32)	Celsius	°C

Weight

1 kilogram	equals	2.2 pounds
500 grams	equals	1.1 pounds
30 grams	equals	1.1 ounce
250 grams	equals	9.0 ounces
100 grams	equals	3.6 ounces

Volume

1 teaspoon	equals	5 milliliters
1 tablespoon	equals	15 milliliters
1/4 cup	equals	62.5 milliliters
1/2 cup	equals	12.5 milliliters
3/4 cup	equals	187.5 milliliters
1 cup	equals	250 milliliters
1.06 pints	equals	500 milliliters
1.06 quarts	equals	1 liter
1.06 gallons	equals	4 liters

Temperature

°C (Celsius)			°F (Fahrenheit)
100	water boils	equals	212
37	body temperature	equals	98.6
0	water freezes	equals	32

A GUIDE TO PURCHASING FOOD FOR FIFTY

A list of some basic and familiar foods used in quantity cooking

FOOD	AMOUNT	MISC. INFORMATION
BEVERAGES		
Coffee	1 to 1 1/2 pounds	6-ounce cup
Tea—hot	2-ounces	6-ounce cup
iced	6 1-ounce bags	12-ounce glass
Juices, fruit for punches	7 46-ounce cans	
Orange juice	5 12-ounce cans	4-ounce glass
Tomato juice	2 No. 10 cans	1/2 cup
BREADS & BAKERY PRODUCTS		
Loaf bread	5 to 6 loaves	1-pound size
Dinner rolls	6 to 8 dozen	
Cakes, angel food & layer	4 to 5 cakes	
CEREAL & CEREAL PRODUCTS		
Corn meal	2 1/2 pounds	
Grits	2 pounds	
Macaroni, spaghetti, rice, & noodles	3 to 4 pounds	
DAIRY PRODUCTS		
Butter & margarine	1 to 1 1/2 pounds	
Cheese, processed	4 to 5 pounds	for sandwiches
Cottage cheese	6 to 7 pounds	for salads
Whipping cream	1 to 1 1/2 quarts	
Coffee cream	1 to 1 1/2 quarts	
Ice cream, in bulk	2 gallons	as a dessert
Milk, a drink	2 1/2 gallons	8-ounce glass
FRUITS, canned	2 to 3 No. 10 cans	as a dessert

MEATS

Beef:
- boneless, pot roast   18 to 20 pounds
- steaks, round   16 to 18 pounds   if boneless
- T-bone   25 pounds
- stew & ground   12 to 15 pounds

Veal:
- cutlets & boneless   14 to 16 pounds
- ground   15 pounds

Fish:
- fillets   14 to 16 pounds
- whole, dressed   35 to 38 pounds
- shrimp, in shell, raw   18 to 20 pounds

Chicken:
- ready-to-cook   18 to 22 pounds

Turkey:
- ready-to-cook   35 to 40 pounds   3-to 4-ounce servings

Pork:
- bacon, sliced   4 1/2 to 5 pounds
- pork chops, loin   14 to 17 pounds
- spareribs   24 to 28 pounds   6-ounce servings
- smoked ham with bone   20 to 22 pounds

Lamb:
- leg roast, bone-in   20 to 24 pounds
- chops   25 pounds   2 each serving

VEGETABLES

- Beans, green   10 to 12 pounds
- Cabbage   12 to 14 pounds
- Carrots   12 to 14 pounds
- Cauliflower   18 to 20 pounds
- Celery for relishes   3 to 4 pounds
- Eggplant   12 to 15 pounds
- Lettuce wedges   8 to 10 heads
-    for garnish-leaf   3 to 4 heads

Potatoes
  to bake   18 to 24 pounds   1 potato each
  to mash   12 to 14 pounds
Sweet potatoes
  to bake   18 to 20 pounds
  to mash   14 to 16 pounds
Squash
  yellow summer   18 to 20 pounds
  zucchini   14 to 16 pounds
Tomatoes for
  slicing   10 pounds
Turnips for
  mashing   12 to 15 pounds

CANNED FOOD

Some commonly used container sizes and equivalents
(Note: One No. 10 can makes approximately 25 servings)

1 No. 10 can	is equal to	7 No. 303 cans (1 lb.)
1 No. 10 can	is equal to	5 No. 2 cans (1 lb. 4 ounces)
1 No. 10 can	is equal to	4 No. 2 1/2 cans (1 lb. 13-ounces)
1 No. 10 can	is equal to	2 No. 3 Cyl (46-to 50-ounces) cans

A GENERAL GUIDE FOR AMOUNTS OF PREPARED FOODS FOR SERVING FIFTY

A list of some basic and familiar foods used in quantity cooking

FOOD	AMOUNT	MISC. INFORMATION
BEVERAGES		
coffee, hot, cocoa	2 1/2 gallons	
iced tea	3 gallons	12-ounce glass
punches	1 3/4 to 2 1/2 gallons	includes refills
BREADS		
regular loaf	5 to 6 loaves	1-pound size
quick breads, loaf	5 to 6 loaves	
yeast dinner rolls	8 dozen, approx.	
biscuits	9 to 10 dozen	
breakfast rolls, sweet	4 1/2 dozen	
corn bread	1 pan 12 x 20 inches	
muffins	8 1/2 dozen	
doughnuts	9 dozen	
CEREAL & CEREAL PRODUCTS		
grits, spaghetti, noodles, & macaroni	2 gallons	
rice, as a vegetable	6 1/2 quarts	
CASSEROLES		
as a side dish	6 1/2 quarts	
main course	3 gallons, approximate	
DESSERTS		
pound & layer cakes	4 to 5 cakes	
sheet cakes	1 pan 12 x 20 x 2 inches	
cookies, small	12 dozen	
pies	8 8-inch pies	cut into 6 wedges each
puddings & gelatin	6 1/2 quarts	

MEATS
- chicken—cubed 5 to 6 pounds
- creamed ham or
  - creamed chicken 6 to 8 quarts
- ham, baked & boiled 9 to 10 pounds
- meat loaf 5 to 6 loaves—average size
- beef stew—main course 3 gallons
- roast beef, boneless 9 pounds

SALADS
- vegetable, bulk 2 gallons
- fruits, fresh 4 1/2 to 5 quarts
- gelatin 6 1/2 quarts
- meat salads 2 gallons, approximate
- potato 6 1/2 quarts

SOUPS
- first course 2 gallons
- main course 3 gallons

VEGETABLES
- creamed and buttered 6 1/2 quarts
- beans, navy & red 7 to 8 1/2 quarts
- potatoes,
  - mashed 6 1/2 quarts
  - baked 1 each
  - pan fried 6 1/2 quarts
  - french fried 14 pounds
  - potato chips 3 pounds

A GUIDE FOR AVERAGE INDIVIDUAL SERVINGS OF PREPARED FOODS

A list of some basic and familiar foods used in quantity cooking

FOOD	AMOUNT	MISC. INFORMATION
BEVERAGES		
coffee, hot tea	6-ounce cup	
iced tea	12-ounce glass	

cocoa, hot chocolate	6-ounce cup	
punches	4 to 5-ounce punch cup	

BREADS
regular loaf	1 to 2 slices
dinner rolls	1 to 2 rolls
breakfast sweet rolls	1 roll
corn breads	2 × 2-inch square

CEREAL & CEREAL PRODUCTS
grits, rice, spaghetti, noodles, & macaroni	1/2 to 3/4 cup

CASSEROLES
side dish	1/2 cup
main course	1 cup

DESSERTS
cakes	2-to 3-ounce slice, or square	
pies	1 wedge from 8-inch pie	cut in 6 wedges
puddings	1/2 cup	
gelatin	1/2 cup	

MEATS
depends on cut, bone, etc	3-to 4-ounce average	steaks & chops larger

SALADS
bulk, vegetable	1/2 to 2/3 cup
gelatin	1/2 cup
potato	1/2 cup
fresh fruit	1/3 to 1/2 cup

SOUPS
first course	1/2 to 2/3 cup
main course	2/3 to 1 1/2 cups

VEGETABLES
creamed & buttered	1/2 cup

SEASONINGS FOR QUANTITY COOKING

There is no phase of food preparation that requires more sensitivity and skill than that of seasonings. To know and understand something of the food habits of the group being fed is very important but not always possible. The cooks should not hesitate to use their ideas for some so-called exotic seasoning if that particular seasoning is in order.

The purpose of seasonings and flavorings is to increase the appeal and the palatability of foods. Seasonings which overpower food can be repulsive. The cooks should take time to experiment ahead with the seasonings—at home, perhaps.

SALT SEASONINGS
  1 to 2 teaspoons salt to 1 pound flour
  1 teaspoon salt to 1 pound meat, except cured meats
  1 teaspoon salt to 1 quart of water for vegetable boiling
  2 teaspoons salt to 1 quart of water for cereals, such as macaroni, noodles, etc.

HERBS AND SPICES

A list of a few familiar and basic foods and suggestions for the herbs and spices which best complement them.

FOODS	HERBS AND SPICES
Cheese soufflé	mustard, paprika, pepper
Fish dishes	thyme, tarragon, dill, bay leaves, almonds, parsley
Fowl; chicken, turkey, etc.	basil, curry powder, paprika, thyme, rosemary, oregano, sage, mace, saffron, and others
Veal	marjoram, allspice, curry powder, saffron, parsley
Lamb	bay leaves, mustard, garlic, curry powder, mint, allspice

Pork	rosemary, caraway, mustard, sage
Ham	sage, cloves, cinnamon, mustard
Beef, pot roast & stew	bay leaves, parsley, cumin, basil, sage, marjoram, parsley
Beef stews, roast, etc.	horseradish, garlic, onion, oregano, mustard, chives, parsley
Wild fowl	sage, thyme, parsley, rosemary, chervil, marjoram
Meat sauces	horseradish, garlic, parsley, bay leaves, thyme, basil, mustard
Vegetables, root	savory, parsley, bay leaves, dill, basil
Vegetables, green	sage, rosemary, thyme, nutmeg, paprika, pepper
Rice	curry powder, saffron, parsley, pepper, lemon
Potatoes	dill, chives, onion, garlic, mint
Salads—not fruits	mustard, garlic, dill, marjoram, curry powder, thyme, chives, onion
Pies	mace, ginger, nutmeg, cinnamon, ground cloves
Puddings	mace, allspice, cloves, nutmeg, cinnamon, flavorings
Fruits, baked	cloves, nutmeg, ginger, cinnamon
Cakes	cloves, nutmeg, cinnamon, cardamon
Cookies	mace, ginger, poppy seed, sesame seed, caraway seed, cardamon
Soups—clear	sherry, sage, chives, basil, tarragon, pepper

Soups—cream	mace, mint, nutmeg, pepper, bay leaves, curry powder
Soups, cold	paprika, pepper, nutmeg, chives
Eggs	turmeric, basil, curry powder, parsley, tarragon
Omelets	curry powder, basil, chives, parsley, marjoram

LEAVENING AGENTS

2 teaspoons soda to 1 quart sour milk
6 teaspoons baking powder to 1 pound flour

THICKENING AGENTS

eggs: 4 to 6 beaten, to 1 quart milk
flour: 2 tablespoons to 1 quart liquid, a very thin sauce
4 tablespoons to 1 quart liquid, medium thick for creamed soups
6 tablespoons to 1 quart liquid, for medium sauce, gravy and vegetable sauces
1/2 cup to 1 quart liquid, a thick sauce

All measures are approximate

OVEN TEMPERATURES FOR BAKING AND ROASTING

very slow oven	250° to 275°
slow oven	300°
moderately slow oven	325°
moderate oven	350°
moderately hot oven	375°
hot oven	400°
very hot oven	450° to 500°

MAKING USE OF CONVENIENCE FOODS IN QUANTITY COOKING

Our present-day culture is so caught up in the do-it-the-easy-fast syndrome in cooking that it is impossible to ignore this dominant trend whether in the home or in quantity cooking. The multitude of prepackaged ready-mixed, frozen, premeasured, precooked (and sometimes I believe "predigested") food offers the cook a shortcut to the finished product.

However, I keep remembering, with nostaglia, the good old-fashioned church suppers (also called dinner-on-the-ground), which were anticipated and planned for days in advance. Mrs. A. would bring her roast chicken with that heavenly dressing, Mrs. B. an elegant meat salad, and Mrs. C. her prize-winning apple pie, all prepared with a labor of uncomplaining love, made in generous amounts. Those were church suppers to remember. I cannot recall a single production that made an impression on me that grew out of a ready-mix package.

My objection to convenience foods is that they take from the cook his or her creative talent. However, there is in the "now" haste and waste culture a need for their use, and we would be unwise not to use them for just what they are—convenience.

The following is a list of convenience foods that I have found especially appropriate for quantity cooking. They seem to hold their flavor and substance well: griddle and waffle mixes; biscuit mixes for dumplings; some cake mixes, such as angel cake, streusel, and pound cakes. Many of the frozen foods are excellent, especially frozen breads baked as directed for a fresh loaf; the gravy and sauce preparations for a hurried meal.

Don't be afraid to spend time and energy preparing food for the crowds by cooking from "scratch." The element of joy and satisfaction of a labor that is creative and adventurous will be a delight that you will long remember.

SERVING THE CROWD

Whether the method of serving is family style, buffet style, the customary seated-and-then-served method, picking up plates from kitchen window or counter that have been served, the most important element of the service is the *manner* in which it is served. The hallmark of courtesy and good manners should be displayed by those attending church suppers.

An orderly, thoughtful, and dignified manner of serving can mean the difference between a meal which is important or one which people would like to forget. To achieve this order and to serve the meal in good taste, I suggest that someone be appointed to act as host or hostess and announce the procedure for the people to be seated or to form a line, depending on what method is being used. Always see that guests go first, then perhaps the elderly of the group, and so on.

The method used for serving a particular meal should be determined by the size of the crowd, the occasion, and the makeup of the crowd, whether it consists of one age level or a mixture. The host or the hostess should be just that from the beginning to the end of the meal.

TASTES AND PREJUDICES

I have long awaited the opportunity to quiet a few of the tired old jokes about church suppers. For years I have been helping in some capacity to serve either church suppers or other large groups, and one of my pet peeves is that somehow and in some manner the church has earned the reputation of serving the same old menu year in and year out, because it "is inexpensive." It has, also, been dull much too often. I have heard many times something like "as dull as a church supper"; or, "as unimaginative as another meal at the church"; or, "Oh, no, not another meal of baked ham with raisin sauce"; or, "I can't face another bowl of carrots and skinny peas"; and on and on—you tell your own!

Now, with some help from the church cooks, I am hoping in this book to create another image, one that says "our church has interesting and delicious food at the church suppers, served with dignity and in good taste," maybe not always inexpensive, but always within bounds. I have left out, on purpose, a few recipes for dishes that are worked to death on quantity menus. If you miss something that you think is standard fare, remember that could be the one thing to forget.

Another one of my prejudices concerns volunteer workers who feel that, since it is just a church crowd, any food can be served on paper plates, with paper cups for coffee and tea, and plastic knives and forks. Obviously, there are many meals that can be served with a paper background, but if time and energy permit, do use china for meals that are hot with gravy or have vegetables with a sauce, and desserts that have a runny syrup over them. And *please* do not use plastic glasses. There are times and circumstances which make it impossible to serve in any other manner than the "paper route," but let that be the exception and not the rule.

About the recipes in this book. I have tried to include enough of the old standard ones with some variations, to make the folks feel at home, and I have included sufficient number of variations on an old theme to interest the groups that are searching for new and exciting menus. But remember, that *there are really no new recipes, only variations on the old theme.* The basic foods remain the same, only the combinations change, or the proportions are switched, and the seasonings and flavorings altered to bring out a different taste.

PART II

POTLUCK SUPPERS

THE POTLUCK SUPPER

More has been said about potluck meals and less written about them than almost any subject that I can think of. It is amazing how little the authors of cookbooks have had to say about this type of meal. Perhaps it is because the potluck meal is either considered too familiar a subject to write about or too vague a subject to inspire either the author or the reader.

The church supper potluck is probably one of the oldest of the potluck meals. Mention is made of potluck suppers in church history when the settlers of New England met for worship and feasting in homes. The meal usually consisted of wild game, baked beans, good breads, and apple pies—all brought to the meeting in generous amounts.

Potluck meals today usually refer to the "bring-whatever-you-have" idea or bring your favorite dish as a contribution to the meal. Many churches now have a part-time cook who prepares a part of the church supper and the church members bring potluck for the remainder of the menu.

In this section you will find some suggestions for planning three different types of the potluck.

AN AUTHENTIC POTLUCK—serving 50

Every church, club, or organization that serves what they call potluck meals should at sometime serve a real one. That is, contributors should bring anything they choose to the meal, be it a meat dish a salad, a vegetable, or a dessert. They should be asked to bring twice the amount needed to feed their family to assure an ample amount of food for all.

Of course, the meal might turn out to be one of all meats, or all salads, or all desserts. What difference does it make if the group eats one meal that is not balanced? I doubt if it would be the first time for many, and may not be the last time. On the other hand, it could be that the meal will have great variety. In fact, the nature of the crowd usually means that each one has his or her favorite dish and will bring just that and duplications will be the exception. LUCK is most often in favor of variety and the POT is sure to be ample.

The drink and the bread could be contributed in a different manner if the food committee wants to make sure about this part of the meal. Those responsible for table and seating preparation might take this portion of the meal as their assignment.

THE PLANNED POTLUCK—serving 50

A *planned potluck* is a misnomer. In this instance, the food committee, after determining the menu, will make special assignments as to what the contributors are to bring to the meal, based on the agreed menu. In order that the assignments may be evenly distributed, as to trouble and expense, it is well to ask for volunteers for certain dishes. After that, ask for definite dishes from those who are dependable in attendance and generous in their sharing.

The division of foods and assignments. Ask five families to bring a meat dish that will *make 10 generous servings,* or *ask ten families* to bring a meat dish that *will* make 5 *generous servings.*

In the same manner assign the salads, vegetables, desserts, and so on.

The drinks, breads, and other items, might be arranged for by the food committee, unless the circumstances call for a complete *planned potluck,* and in that instance continue the assignment of five for this or that, or ten for this or that.

Here are three suggested menus for *planned potluck* church suppers to serve 50.

1. **A MEAT LOAF SUPPER**
   5 average-size meat loaves
   potatoes au gratin
   cabbage salad
   relish plates
   French bread, 5 or 6 loaves
   5 cakes, an assortment

2. **A BAKED HAM SUPPER**
   50 generous slices of baked ham
   sweet potatoes, en casserole
   fruit salads
   hot rolls, 7 or 8 dozen
   8 pies, an assortment

3. **MEAT BALLS AND SPAGHETTI SUPPER**
   5 bowls of meat balls & spaghetti sufficient to make 10 servings each or 10 bowls sufficient to serve 5 persons each
   lettuce salad, tossed with oil & vinegar dressing
   French bread, 5 or 6 loaves
   peach cobbler or an assortment of cobblers

THE SUPPLEMENTED POTLUCK SUPPER—to serve 50

Many large churches now have a full-time or a part-time cook who prepares the main dish, the drink, and the bread, and the members bring the remainder of the menu. This type of supper needs planning just as the other types of meals; the difference is, of course, that this type requires less food. However, the members are expected to pay for the portion prepared at the church in addition to bringing the remainder of the menu.

For that portion which is contributed by the members follow the plan as given for the *planned potluck* meal.

The two suggested menus for this supplemented potluck given here are popular and easy to prepare.

1. **ROAST TURKEY**
    dressing or stuffing to be determined by the church cook, and cooked at the church with the turkey
    cranberry sauce
    fruit salads
    baked corn en casserole
    hot rolls, 7 or 8 dozen
    5 cakes, an assortment

2. **FRIED CHICKEN**
    mashed potatoes
    cole slaw, cabbage with a cooked dressing
    loaf breads, served hot
    5 chocolate cakes

PART III

TRADITIONAL AND NEW RECIPES

TRADITIONAL AND NEW RECIPES

APPETIZERS

Although a cookbook such as this may not call for a section on appetizers, I am listing here a few suggestions that may be of help to the cooks who find that on occasion these are a delightful addition to the menu. Also, a time may come when an entire meal of hors d'oeuvres, canapes, relishes, broths, or some other appetizers is in order.

A large platter or tray with an arrangement of:

1. Carrot curls; celery rings; deviled eggs; tiny smoked sausages; tiny sandwiches of bread and butter, and radish roses in center for garnish.

2. An assortment of fresh fruits and melon chunks; cheese wafers; tuna salad in lettuce cups; olives, celery sticks.

3. Cheese spreads, heavily seasoned and on a canapé base of toasted bread rounds; marinated fresh cucumber sticks; avocado dip in lettuce cups.

4. Sweet and sour wieners (see recipe), cut into small rounds; pickles; olives; thin slices of ham wrapped around marinated asparagus tips; tiny sandwiches of rye bread and butter.

5. An assortment of melon chunks; small cream puffs filled with chicken salad; cheese wafers; pickled peach halves; ripe olives.

6. A huge dip of blue cheese, sour cream, and cream cheese, seasoned with grated onion and Jalapeño peppers and surrounded by tiny squares of toasted French bread. Radishes, cucumbers, olives, and carrot sticks may be used for the decoration or garnish.

BEVERAGES

Coffee

Coffee is perhaps the most universally consumed of all hot beverages. To be really good, coffee should be freshly made and when possible, served immediately. For large amounts this is rarely possible. All coffee-making utensils should be kept clean and when not in use, kept in a place where fresh air can circulate in and around them. To freshen a coffee-making utensil rinse it with fresh water, adding 2 or 3 tablespoons of baking soda to the rinse water. This helps to prevent, and to remove, the rancid taste that often affects the pot after much use.

Most coffee companies now furnish the container and the recipes when the coffee is purchased in large amounts. For those church kitchens that do not have this service, I am giving some recipes using different methods.

STEEPED COFFEE

Obviously, this is not a very practical way to make coffee for a large crowd; however, it is a wonderful way to make it for a small group, when the coffee-making can become a part of the evening's program. Making it by this method can add an atmosphere of camaraderie to a small group meeting. Doughnuts and steeped coffee could be the order of the meeting.

When making it, allow 2 tablespoons coffee and 1 or 1 1/2 cups boiling water for each finished cup of coffee. Add one-half of one eggshell for every three or four cups of coffee, and a sprinkle of salt for each cup. Into a suitable container, earthenware preferred, pour the boiling water over the coffee grounds, add salt and eggshell, cover with a tight lid, and steep for 4 or 5 minutes. Strain and drink immediately. This coffee has a very special flavor.

DRIP COFFEE

Many of the coffee makers furnished by coffee companies are for drip coffee, and with the coffee maker comes the recipe. But for those who do not have this service, I suggest the following recipe.

To make 50 servings, 6-ounce cups (with a few refills)

YOU WILL NEED 1 1/4 pounds drip-grind coffee
2 1/2 to 3 gallons boiling water

THE PREPARATION

Make sure the utensil is clean and the coffee the correct grind. Place the coffee in the section of the pot designed for it, then pour the boiling water through slowly. When 2 1/2 gallons of boiling water have been poured over the grounds, test for strength. If too strong, add about 1/2 gallon more water.

PERCOLATED COFFEE

This is the method used most often in quantity cooking, and the coffee maker for this method is usually furnished by the coffee company when their brand of coffee is purchased. The recipe comes with the coffee maker. But for those who do not have a recipe, you are safe in making coffee for 50 by using 1 to 1 1/2 pounds of regular or percolator grind coffee with 2 1/2 to 3 gallons of water. Set the strength control before turning the electricity on.

CAFÉ AU LAIT

The famous French coffee is truly worth all of the expense and extra trouble that seems necessary to prepare it. The real New Orleans method of serving this delightful drink is to use both hands at the same time, pouring into the cup hot cream with one hand and hot coffee with the other. It is quite a trick, but adds tremendous interest and conversation for any group gathering. This is the perfect time to serve creole doughnuts (see recipe, P. 85). Cut them in squares, serve with cafe au lait. Have a bowl of powdered sugar handy to dip hot doughnuts in, then dunk them into the hot coffee. Delicious.

To make this coffee for 50 servings

YOU WILL NEED
1 pound coffee, proper grind for utensil being used
1 3/4 gallons boiling water
1 1/2 gallons half and half cream (or milk and some cream)
powdered sugar (optional)

THE PREPARATION

Use whatever utensil is available to make a strong coffee. Heat the cream and keep it hot by setting the kettle of cream in a large pan of hot water. It should be heated only to scald, never boiled. When serving this drink with powdered sugar, no other sugar will be needed.

COFFEE
Picnic-style

I like to call this method bag coffee since the grounds are placed in a cheesecloth bag and dropped into a large kettle of boiling water. This method is considered by some as having the most pleasant taste of all, perhaps because it is often made in open country, over an open fire, and the aroma it gives off is long remembered.

To make about 50 servings

YOU WILL NEED

1 pound regular grind coffee
2 1/2 to 3 gallons boiling water
cheesecloth, about 36 inches square
1 eggshell
1 teaspoon salt

THE PREPARATION

First, tie the coffee securely in the cheesecloth with a strong string. Place the bag in a large kettle of boiling water. Be sure there is room for boiling *and* the bag. Allow the water to boil for about 10 minutes. While it is boiling, punch and push the bag with a wooden spoon to bring out the essence. When the color of the water is the strength you are seeking, add the eggshell and salt. Cover and set aside for about 15 minutes, or until the coffee clears. Taste for strength. It can be reheated without loss of flavor, in fact, sometimes the flavor is enhanced by reheating—especially out in the country.

ICED COFFEE

When serving iced coffee to 50 people, make a full recipe of strong coffee ahead and freeze in cubes, or in some desired shape that is easy to handle. This can be done days in advance, by freezing small amounts and removing them to freezer bags until the full amount is completed. A whole clove can be frozen in each cube of coffee for a delightful change and a surprise flavor. When ready to use, make a full recipe of fresh hot coffee, fill 12-ounce glasses with the frozen coffee cubes and pour the coffee over these while it is still warm. Have cream and sugar available for those who wish them.

> The discovery of a new dish does more for the happiness of man than the discovery of a new star.
> —Brillat-Savarin

CHOCOLATE-COFFEE

To make approximately 50 servings of 6 ounces each

YOU WILL NEED
- 1 1/2 gallons strong hot coffee
- 2 quarts boiling water
- 2 quarts hot milk
- 1 pint coffee cream
- 1 1/2 cups sugar
- 1/2 cup cocoa, or 5 ounces melted unsweetened chocolate
- 2 teaspoons vanilla
- 1/2 teaspoon nutmeg
- 1/4 teaspoon salt

THE PREPARATION

Add the sugar, cocoa, or melted chocolate to the boiling water, and stir until blended. Scald the milk and cream, but do not boil. Stir in the flavorings and salt, adjusting the flavorings to suit the taste and combine the mixtures with the hot coffee. Serve at once if serving as a hot drink, or make ahead and chill to serve as a cold drink. For something special top each cup of the drink with a teaspoon of whipped cream, sprinkled with nutmeg. This can be served as an after-dinner drink.

Tea

Those who insist on serving instant tea can follow the directions on the container to determine the quantity, but I do *not* recommend instant tea for any occasion.

HOT TEA

The best method of serving hot tea is in an individual earthenware teapot with a single tea bag that makes 1 or 2 cups only. But there are times when tea needs be made in large amounts, especially for parties. For that, use the following recipe.

To make approximately 50 servings

YOU WILL NEED
- 3 or 4 1-ounce tea bags
- 2 1/2 gallons boiling water
- sugar
- lemon

THE PREPARATION

Hot tea is greatly affected by the container in which it is made. A large earthenware container, with a lid to cover it while the tea is steeping, adds to the flavor and to the color. If this type of container is not available use enamel or stainless steel. Pour the boiling water into the container, drop in the tea bags, and steep for about 10 minutes. Test during the steeping to get the desired strength. It is best served immediately. Reheating tea darkens it, although I have done it occasionally without much loss of color or flavor. Have sugar and lemon slices available.

ICED TEA

Make a stronger tea for iced tea than for hot tea. Make it just as near serving time as possible for best results. Pour it into a 12-ounce glass filled with ice cubes while it is still warm or very fresh. Serve with sugar and lemon wedges and when possible with fresh mint leaves. A most refreshing drink.

Chocolate Drinks

HOT CHOCOLATE
French-style

Although this drink is usually served as a party refreshment, it can be served with a light meal at a church supper. It is rich and satisfying.

To make 50 generous servings

YOU WILL NEED
- 1 pound unsweetened chocolate
- 3 cups hot water
- 5 cups sugar, or less
- 1/2 teaspoon salt
- 1 quart whipping cream
- 2 1/2 gallons milk, scalded

THE PREPARATION

Combine the chocolate with the hot water and cook slowly over direct heat, stirring constantly until melted and well blended. Add sugar and salt and return to heat, over hot water, and cook until the sugar has dissolved and the mixture is thick. Chill or refrigerate until ready to use. When ready to make the drink, scald the milk and combine with the chocolate mixture. Cook slowly over low heat, stirring until well blended. Whip the cream and just before serving fold the cream into the mixture. Serve at once. The whipped cream can be used to garnish each separate cup as it is being served. Sprinkle with shredded chocolate.

HOT COCOA
Old-Fashioned

When an inexpensive chocolate drink is in order, or when it is necessary to plan for refills, I find this drink the answer. It goes especially well on a cold winter night for a group of teenagers, or with a meal of snacks.

To make approximately 50 generous servings

YOU WILL NEED
- 1 1/2 cups cocoa
- 3 cups sugar
- 1/4 teaspoon salt
- 1 quart hot water
- 2 1/4 gallons hot milk
- marshmallows for top (optional)

THE PREPARATION

Add the cocoa, sugar, and salt to the hot water and cook over low heat until the mixture is blended and smooth, and thick enough to be syrupy—about 10 minutes or a little longer. Stir while cooking. Scald the milk, but do not boil, and combine the mixtures. Keep hot until ready to serve. A marshmallow placed on the top of each cup as it is being served adds substance as well as appetite appeal.

VARIATION

For a different flavor, add 2 tablespoons orange flavoring just before taking the mixture from the heat.

Punches

Frozen fruit punch in concentrated form can be found now in several flavors and in combinations of flavors in most supermarkets. The directions on these can be followed easily and the results are very good.

Serving punch. The average punch cup holds 4 ounces. The cup should never be completely filled, since most "punch-drinking" parties are dress-up affairs, and most people stand.

FRUIT PUNCH
a basic recipe

An excellent foundation punch can be made with countless variations. I give here only a few, but with a bit of imagination the cook can come up with a delicious cold or hot drink using combinations yet untried. The cook might do well to keep a syrup made ahead and stored for sweetening punches when the need arises. To make this syrup use 1 quart water with 4 to 6 cups of sugar. Combine and cook until smooth and thick.

Chill and store. Add to punches in amounts needed. The following recipe for 2 1/2 gallons will make 100 punch-cup servings of 4-ounces each.

To make this foundation punch

YOU WILL NEED
- 5 to 6 cups sugar, depending on tartness of juices
- 1 quart of hot water
- 2 12-ounce cans frozen orange juice
- 2 12-ounce cans frozen lemon juice
- 1 6-ounce can frozen lime juice
- 2 gallons cold water

THE PREPARATION

Add the sugar to the hot water and cook for 5 or 6 minutes, until the sugar is dissolved. Chill. Add the frozen juices to the cold water and stir until blended. The syrup should be added gradually and the mixture tasted to get the correct sweetness. Chill thoroughly before serving. If possible, have a large chunk of ice in the bowl and pour the punch over it.

VARIATIONS

Raspberry punch. Reduce the lemon juice to 1 6-ounce can and the orange juice to 1 12-ounce can and add 2 12-ounce packages of frozen raspberries and 1 quart of chilled ginger ale to the mixture. Prepare and serve as directed.

Apricot punch. Reduce the orange juice to 1 12-ounce can, omit the lime juice, add 2 46-ounce cans of apricot nectar and 1 quart of chilled ginger ale. Prepare and serve as directed.

Grape punch. Reduce the orange juice to 1 12-ounce can, omit the lime juice, and add 1 24-ounce can frozen grape juice and 1 quart of chilled ginger ale. Prepare and serve as directed.

Some of these variations will not measure out exactly to 2 1/2 gallons but the differences are not significant.

ORANGE-CIDER PUNCH

To make 100 servings

YOU WILL NEED
- 2 gallons hot apple cider
- 1 quart orange juice (fresh or made from frozen)
- 1 quart strong tea
- 1 to 2 cups sugar
- 2 tablespoons whole cloves, in cloth bag

THE PREPARATION

Bring the cider and tea to a boil, add sugar and set off the heat. Drop in cloves bag and with a wooden spoon press it to extract a strong flavor. Stir in orange juice and reheat the mixture if serving hot. The punch can be chilled and served cold.

THE WITCH'S PUNCH
a Halloween drink

The title creates the atmosphere—spooks like this drink.

To make 25 generous servings

YOU WILL NEED
- 2 1/2 quarts strong tea
- 2 1/2 quarts apple cider
- 1/2 cup brown sugar, or a little more
- 1 tablespoon whole cloves, broken into tiny bits

THE PREPARATION

Mix all of the ingredients together and serve hot or cold, depending on the occasion or the weather. When serving cold, add one bottle of chilled ginger ale. It can also be served as the drink for a church supper instead of the usual tea or coffee, providing the menu corresponds.

HOT SPICED TEA

To make approximately 50 servings

YOU WILL NEED
- 1/2 cup, or a little less, bulk tea
- 1 1/2 gallons boiling water
- 10 cinnamon sticks
- 2 tablespoons whole cloves
- 1/2 cup lemon juice
- 2 cups orange concentrate
- 4 to 5 cups sugar

THE PREPARATION

Drop the tea into the boiling water, cover and set aside to steep. Add the cloves, cinnamon, and sugar. Stir well until blended and the sugar has dissolved. When the tea reaches the desired strength, strain the mixture. Add the lemon and orange juices and stir again. Reheat before serving.

LIME-SHERBET PUNCH

We usually think of this punch as a party refreshment, but there are times when it can be served as a dessert, that is, if the meal has been a light one. To serve as a dessert make it at the last minute, fill the punch cups to 3/4 full, place on a tray and pass to guests.

To make approximately 50 servings

YOU WILL NEED
- 3 quarts lime sherbet
- 3 quarts chilled ginger ale
- 1/3 cup lemon juice

THE PREPARATION

Sprinkle the lemon juice over the bottom of a chilled punch bowl. Spoon the sherbet into the bowl and pour the chilled ginger ale over it, breaking it up slightly as the ale is being added. When filling the punch cups make sure that both the ale and the sherbet are a part of the serving.

VARIATIONS

Instead of lime sherbet use an equal amount of raspberry sherbet, strawberry sherbet, lemon sherbet or cherry ice cream.

COFFEE PUNCH

To serve this exotic punch for teas and parties with a special bit of glamor, add a spoonful of whipped cream to the top of each serving and sprinkle a little shredded chocolate on top. This slows down the serving and takes extra time and energy, but it is impressive. It also gets cream on the upper lip and nose but at the same time makes for a conversation topic.

To make 50 generous punch-cup servings

YOU WILL NEED

4 quarts freshly made strong coffee chilled (never instant coffee)
4 quarts vanilla ice cream
2 quarts heavy cream, whipped and slightly sweetened
1 cup crème de cacao (optional)
shredded unsweetened chocolate for garnish

THE PREPARATION

Make the coffee ahead and chill. Also whip the cream to a stiff peak, sweeten with about 1/2 cup powdered sugar, and chill. Chill a large punch bowl, and place 2 quarts of the ice cream in the cold bowl. Pour 2 quarts, or a little more, of the chilled coffee over the ice cream and a generous amount of the whipped cream on the top. If using crème de cacao, add some at this point. The shredded chocolate can be added now also. When this portion of the punch has been used, repeat the process. Make sure each serving has a portion of each of the ingredients in the cup. This punch can be served at wedding receptions with tremendous success.

HOT SPICED TOMATO JUICE

This juice is a good appetizer before a meal of pasta, or before a meal consisting of a casserole as the main course.

To make approximately 50 generous servings

YOU WILL NEED
- 3 46-ounce cans tomato juice (about 4 quarts)
- 3/4 cup finely chopped onion
- 1 cup finely chopped celery
- 2 bay leaves
- 1 tablespoon allspice
- 6 whole cloves
- 1 gallon chicken consommé, made of 2 quarts condensed chicken consommé and 2 quarts water
- 1 teaspoon Tabasco sauce, more or less
- Salt

THE PREPARATION

In a large kettle combine the tomato juice and the seasonings, except salt. Place over low heat and simmer for about 20 minutes or until the flavors are blended. Press the mixture through a strainer with a wooden spoon and combine with the consommé. Return to the heat and simmer again for about 10 minutes. Taste for salt, and add only if needed. The consommé will have added to the salt flavor already. Stir in the Tabasco sauce gradually, and taste for desired amount. Serve by pouring from a large preheated pitcher.

BREAD

Bread has been a part of man's history from the beginning of his recorded existence. Man's physical life has been dependent on this necessity since his creation. Whatever the translation of the word might be, the significance of its meaning remains the same—life's sustaining nourishment.

Since bread has always held such an important place in our physical existence and has been referred to over and over as the *bread of life,* it seems only natural that church suppers should make this food an important part of menus. I would like to challenge the church cooks to return to baking bread for church suppers. From my years of experience with bread baking, I know that the aroma from a good loaf of bread baking will inspire the entire crowd to rise up and call the bread baker *blessed.* No food, no matter how beautiful or tasty, gives the satisfaction that a piece of good freshly baked bread does.

WHITE BREAD
a basic recipe

If the size of the crowd calls for more bread than this one recipe, do not double it, but make the recipe twice.

To make 4 medium loaves (approximately 1 pound each)

YOU WILL NEED	2 packages active dry yeast 1 cup lukewarm water 6 tablespoons sugar 1 tablespoon salt 5 tablespoons shortening 1 egg 2 1/2 cups milk, scalded 7 to 8 1/2 cups all-purpose flour

THE PREPARATION

In a large saucepan scald the milk and, while it is still hot, add the shortening, salt, and sugar. Stir well and set aside to cool. (If time is of great importance, cool the mixture by placing the saucepan in a larger pan of ice or cold water.) Dissolve the yeast in the lukewarm water and set aside. When the milk has cooled to lukewarm, combine the two mixtures. Beat in the egg and begin adding the flour. Beat in the flour little by little, either by hand or in an electric mixer. When the dough becomes too thick to beat, add a little more flour, by mixing with hands. When the dough has reached a moderately firm stage, but is still pliable and elastic, turn it into a large, deep, greased bowl. Turn over once to grease the top. Cover and set aside, out of drafts, and let rise until doubled in bulk, about 1 to 1 1/2 hours.

When the dough has doubled in bulk, punch it down to its original size, cover, and let rise again until doubled in bulk, about 1 hour. This second rising is not always necessary and, if time is limited, it can be omitted. However, it does add to the lightness of the loaf.

After the dough has doubled the second time, turn it out onto a floured surface, knead slightly and form into four equal loaves, and knead each of them slightly. Place them in well-greased loaf pans, cover, and let rise until doubled in bulk, about 1 hour. When ready to bake, brush the loaves with melted butter, or margarine, and bake in a preheated oven at 375° for about 35 minutes. Or bake until the loaves are brown and pulled slightly from the sides of the pans. Another test for doneness is to thump the loaves with the fingers, and if the loaves sound hollow, they are done. For a soft tasty crust, brush the loaves again with melted butter as they come from the oven. Cool on a wire rack.

VARIATION

For making dinner rolls with this recipe see the the Yeast Bread Roll recipe, p. 68.

WHOLE WHEAT BREAD
a basic recipe

To make 4 medium loaves

YOU WILL NEED

2 packages active dry yeast
1 cup lukewarm water
2 1/2 cups milk, scalded
1 tablespoon salt
1/2 cup dark molasses
6 tablespoons shortening
1 egg
3 cups whole wheat flour, stone-ground, if possible
5 1/2 to 6 1/2 cups all-purpose flour

THE PREPARATION

Scald the milk and while it is still hot add the salt, shortening, molasses and stir until well blended. Set aside. Dissolve the yeast in the lukewarm water and set aside. When the milk mixture has cooled to lukewarm, stir in the egg and combine the two mixtures. Start adding the flours (which have been sifted and resifted)—first the whole wheat, then the all-purpose, beating either by hand or with an electric mixer. Keep beating and adding until the dough becomes too thick to beat, then add more of the all-purpose with the hands. Add sufficient to make a firm dough which is still pliable and elastic. Place in a deep, well-greased bowl, and turn once to grease the top. Cover and set aside to rise until doubled in bulk. About 1 to 1 1/2 hours.

When the dough has doubled, punch it down to its original size, cover and let rise again until doubled, about 1 hour.

After it has doubled the second time, turn it out onto a floured surface, knead slightly and form into four equal loaves. Knead each loaf slightly, using extra flour if necessary to handle easily. Place in well-greased loaf pans, cover and let rise until doubled in bulk, about 1 hour.

When the loaves have doubled, brush them with melted butter or margarine and bake in a preheated oven at 375° for about 35 minutes or until brown and pulled slightly from the sides of the pans. When the bread is done, it should sound hollow when thumped with the fingers. For a soft, rich crust, brush the loaves again with melted butter or margarine as they come from the oven. Cool on a rack. See recipe for freezing bread, and see recipe for making rolls, using whole wheat basic recipe.

FRENCH BREAD

These long thin loaves are slightly tough, chewy with crisp crusts, and of a porous texture. French bread is one of the most sought after of all breads, whether it is made at home or at the bakery in the old-fashioned European style, with special equipment. To make 50 servings of this recipe repeat it once, instead of doubling it. The unbleached flour in this recipe gives it a special flavor.

To make two long, thin loaves

YOU WILL NEED
- 1 package active dry yeast
- 1 1/2 cups lukewarm water
- 2 teaspoons salt
- 1 tablespoon sugar
- 3 tablespoons shortening, melted
- 4 to 5 cups, unbleached white flour
- cornmeal for pan
- 1 beaten egg to brush top

THE PREPARATION

Dissolve the yeast in lukewarm water and set aside. In a large mixing bowl, sift 4 cups of the flour with the salt and sugar. Stir until well blended. Add the dissolved yeast and the melted shortening and beat either by hand or with an electric mixer. When the dough becomes too thick to beat, add more flour by mixing with the hands. Add sufficient flour to make a firm dough but one that is still pliable. Turn out onto a floured surface and knead for about 10 minutes, then place in a greased bowl, cover and set aside to rise until doubled in bulk, about 1 1/2 hours.

After the dough has doubled turn it out again on the floured surface. Divide into two equal parts and knead each part thoroughly, about 5 or 10 minutes for each part, adding flour as necessary to make the dough hold its shape. Form the parts into long, tapered loaves. Place on a greased baking sheet which has been sprinkled with cornmeal. Leave space between the loaves for expansion in order for them to be crusty on all sides. They should not touch. Cut diagonal slashes across the tops of each loaf, about 1/2-inch deep and about 2-inches long and at 3 or 4-inch intervals. Brush the loaves with a mixture of one beaten egg and 1 tablespoon warm water. Set the bread aside to rise again, uncovered, until doubled, about 1 1/2 hours. Bake in a preheated oven at 400° for about 15 minutes or until the loaves are slightly brown, then reduce the heat to 350° and continue baking for about 30 minutes longer, or until the bread is brown and sounds hollow when thumped with the fingers. Cool on a wire rack.

RYE BREAD

A church supper, or any church meal for that matter consisting of cold cuts, hot potato salad, cheeses, and plenty of freshly made rye bread could be a meal to long remember. This loaf can be made in advance, frozen, then reheated and served tasting as fresh as when it came from the oven the first time. Then you could say "churchmade bread," not "homemade." These loaves can be cut into about 20 slices each. To make 50 generous servings make this recipe twice.

To make 3 long, thin loaves

YOU WILL NEED
2 packages active dry yeast
1 1/2 cups lukewarm water
1/2 cup dark molasses
1 tablespoon salt
2 tablespoons caraway seed (optional)
1 cup milk
4 tablespoons shortening
2 cups rye flour, stone-ground
1 cup whole wheat flour, stone-ground
4 to 5 cups unbleached white flour
cornmeal for pan

For top:
1 teaspoon instant coffee crystals
3 tablespoons hot water

THE PREPARATION

Scald the milk and while it is still hot add the molasses, salt, and shortening, and set aside to cool. Dissolve the yeast in the warm water and when the milk mixture is cool combine the two mixtures. Stir in the caraway seed and start beating in the flours—first the rye, then the whole wheat, and enough of the unbleached to make a very firm dough. When the dough becomes too thick to beat, add more of the unbleached flour by mixing with the hands. Rye and whole wheat flours are inclined to make the dough very sticky, but if you keep the hands dusted with the unbleached flour you will find the dough is much easier to manage.

Place the dough on a floured surface and knead for about 10 minutes or longer, adding more flour if necessary to make a very firm dough. Turn the dough into a deep, well-greased bowl, cover and set aside to rise until doubled in bulk, about 1 1/2 hours.

When the dough has doubled, turn it out onto a floured surface again and divide into three equal parts. Knead each part for about 5 minutes, then form the parts into long, tapered loaves. Place on greased baking sheets which have been generously sprinkled with cornmeal. Cut diagonal slashes across the top of each loaf, about 3-inches apart and about 2-inches in length. Brush the loaves with a mixture of the coffee and hot water. Let rise again, uncovered, until doubled in bulk, about 1 1/2 hours. Bake in a preheated oven at 350° for about 45 minutes or until brown and the loaves sound hollow when thumped with the fingers. Remove to a cooling rack.

PUMPERNICKEL

Anyone who has made loaf bread can make this, or the beginner with an adventurous spirit can make it. It is a bit detailed, with a few more ingredients than the average bread, but really just as easy to make. The loaf is rather dense, but fine textured and with a full flavor. Serve it with pot roast, cold cuts, cheeses, or meat salads.

Each of these 3 loaves can be cut into about 20 thin slices. To make 50 generous servings, repeat the recipe once.

> Nor fresh, nor old be bread but spongy light
> Tasteful, baked of wheat and freed from all blight.
> —School of Salerno Code of Health
> 11th century

To make 3 long, narrow loaves

YOU WILL NEED

3 packages active dry yeast
1 1/2 cups lukewarm water
1 cup milk
1 tablespoon salt
1/2 cup dark molasses
2 tablespoons caraway seed
4 tablespoons shortening
1 tablespoon cocoa & 1 teaspoon instant coffee crystals dissolved in 1/3 cup hot water
2 cups rye flour
1/2 cup bran flour, or buckwheat
1 3/4 cups whole wheat flour
3 cups, or more, unbleached white flour
cornmeal for pan

For top:
2 teaspoons instant coffee crystals
3 tablespoons hot water
poppy seed

THE PREPARATION

Scald the milk and, while it is still hot, add the shortening, molasses, salt and set aside to cool. In 1/3 cup hot water dissolve the cocoa and instant coffee crystals and set aside. Dissolve the yeast in the lukewarm water and, when the milk has cooled to room temperature, combine all three mixtures. Stir in the caraway seed and start beating in the flours—first the rye, then the other dark flours. Beat either by hand or with electric mixer. When the dark flours are well blended, start adding the unbleached. If the dough becomes too thick to beat, add more of the unbleached flour by mixing with the hands. Add sufficient flour to make a very firm but still pliable dough. Turn the dough out onto a floured surface and knead vigorously for 10 or 15 minutes, adding more unbleached flour if needed. Place in a deep, well-greased bowl, turn once to grease the top, cover and set aside to rise until doubled in bulk, about 1 1/2 hours. (The dark flours are heavier than the white and thus the extra yeast is needed, and sometimes the rising time is longer. It may take 2 hours for the dough to double.) When the dough has doubled, turn it out again onto a floured surface and divide into three equal parts. Knead each part for about 5 minutes, adding flour if necessary, then shape each part into a long, narrow, tapered loaf. Place the loaves on baking sheet, or sheets, which have been greased and sprinkled with cornmeal. Cut diagonal slashes across the tops of the loaves about 2-inches in length and about 3-inches apart. Brush them with a mixture of the instant coffee and hot water, and sprinkle generously with poppy seed. Set aside, uncovered, and let rise again until doubled in bulk, about 1 1/2 hours. Bake in a preheated oven at 400° for about 15 minutes, then reduce the heat to 350° and bake for about 35 minutes longer, or until the bread sounds hollow when thumped with the fingers. Cool on a wire rack. This bread, like all of the others given here, freezes well and can be sliced, reheated, and eaten without loss of flavor or texture.

ONION & COTTAGE CHEESE
with Whole Wheat

To make 3 medium loaves

YOU WILL NEED

- 2 packages active dry yeast
- 2/3 cup lukewarm water
- 2 cups cottage cheese, sieved
- 2 tablespoons grated fresh onion
- 4 tablespoons shortening, melted
- 1 tablespoon salt
- 3 tablespoons honey
- 1 tablespoon dark brown sugar
- 2 eggs
- 1/2 teaspoon soda
- 2 cups whole wheat flour, stone-ground
- 3 to 4 1/2 cups all-purpose flour

THE PREPARATION

Prepare the cottage cheese ahead by running it through a sieve or a blender. It should be very smooth and creamy. Dissolve the yeast in the warm water and combine with the cheese. Stir in the onion, salt, sugar, honey, eggs, and shortening. Stir until well blended. Sift the soda with some of the flour and add it to the mixture. Beat in the flours, either by hand or with electric mixer, starting first with the whole wheat, then the all-purpose. When the dough becomes too thick to beat, add more of the all-purpose flour by mixing it in with the hands. The dough should be firm but still soft and elastic. The dough will be quite sticky, so keep the hands dusted with flour and work fast to make the dough manageable.

Turn the dough into a large, deep, well-greased bowl, and turn once to grease the top. Cover and set aside to rise until doubled in bulk, about 1 1/2 hours. When it has doubled, punch it down to its original size and let it rise again until doubled, about 1 hour.

After the dough has doubled the second time, turn it out onto a floured surface, divide into three equal parts, knead each slightly, and add a little flour if necessary to make the handling easy. Form into loaves and place in well-greased loaf pans. Cover and set aside to rise again until doubled in bulk, about 1 hour. Brush them with melted butter and bake in a preheated oven at 375° for about 35 minutes, or until brown and pulled slightly from the sides of the pans. Brush again with melted butter when removing from oven. These are rich, crusty loaves and delicious!

VARIATION

To make cheese whole-wheat rolls. When this dough has doubled the first time, divide it into small parts for easy handling. Roll out to about 1/2-inch thickness. With a biscuit cutter, cut into about 2 to 2 1/2-inch rounds, dip each in melted butter, fold in the center, and press the edges together firmly. Place in a shallow, greased baking pan, cover, and let rise for about 20 minutes. Bake at 400° for about 20 minutes, or until brown. Brush again with melted butter when the rolls have been removed from the oven. These can be frozen and later thawed and reheated without loss of flavor or texture. A very popular roll.

DILL AND ONION BREAD

You will find this bread nutritious, tasty, light, and well textured. It is an excellent one to serve for luncheons and brunches as well as for suppers. This recipe makes three medium loaves, and each one can be cut into 14 or more slices. To make 50 generous servings repeat the recipe once.

To make 3 medium loaves

YOU WILL NEED

2 packages active dry yeast
3/4 cup lukewarm water
2 cups cottage cheese, sieved
2 tablespoons grated fresh onion
2 1/2 tablespoons dill seed
2 tablespoons sugar
2 teaspoons salt
4 tablespoons melted butter or margarine
2 eggs
1/2 teaspoon soda
6 to 7 cups all-purpose flour

THE PREPARATION

Prepare the cottage cheese ahead by running it through a sieve or a blender. It should be very smooth and creamy. Dissolve the yeast in the lukewarm water and combine with the cheese. Stir in the eggs, onion, sugar, shortening, salt and dill seed. Start beating in the flour, either by hand or with electric mixer. Sift the soda with a portion of the flour before beating it in. Continue adding flour until the dough reaches a firm stage, but is still soft. When the dough becomes too thick to beat, add more flour by mixing with hands. The combination of ingredients in this mixture will be very sticky. Keep the hands dusted with flour to make the handling easier. Place the dough in a deep, well-greased bowl, cover and set aside to rise until doubled in bulk, about 1 1/2 hours.

When the dough has doubled, turn it out onto a floured surface and knead slightly, adding more flour if needed for easy handling. Divide it into three equal parts, and form each into a loaf. Place the loaves into well-greased loaf pans, cover and set aside to rise again until doubled in bulk, about 1 hour. When the loaves are ready to bake, brush them with melted butter and bake in a preheated oven at 375° for about 35 minutes or until brown and pulled slightly away from the sides of the pans. For a soft, tasty crust, brush again as they come from the oven. Cool on a wire rack.

RAISIN BREAD

A slice of this bread, buttered and served hot, with jars of jams and jellies scattered around on the tables, makes an excellent dessert for a Church Supper. Try it! This recipe makes 3 medium loaves and each can be cut into about 16 slices. To make 50 generous servings repeat the recipe once.

To make 3 medium loaves

YOU WILL NEED
- 2 packages active dry yeast
- 1 cup lukewarm water
- 1 1/2 cups milk
- 1/2 cup sugar
- 1/2 cup butter
- 2 eggs
- 2 teaspoon salt
- 1 cup raisins, dusted in flour
- 7 to 8 cups all-purpose flour

THE PREPARATION

Scald the milk and while it is still hot add the butter, sugar and salt. Set aside to cool. Dissolve the yeast in the warm water and when the milk has cooled to lukewarm, combine the two mixtures. Stir in the eggs, and start beating in the flour, little by little. Beat either by hand or with an electric mixer. Add the raisins, which have been dusted with flour. Mix with the hands to distribute the raisins evenly. Continue adding flour, either by beating or with hands until the dough is quite firm but still soft. Turn into a deep, well-greased bowl, cover and set aside to rise until doubled in bulk, about 1 1/2 hours.

When it has doubled, punch it down to its original size, and if it is rather sticky, add a little more flour by mixing with the hands. Cover and set aside again to rise until doubled in bulk, about 1 hour.

After the dough has doubled the second time, turn it out onto a floured surface, and knead slightly, use a little flour if necessary to make the handling easy. Divide it into 3 equal parts, and form each into a loaf. Place in well greased loaf pans, cover and let rise again until doubled in bulk, about 1 hour.

When ready to bake, brush them with melted butter and bake in a preheated oven at 375° for about 35 minutes or until the bread is brown and pulled away from the sides of the pans. Brush again with melted butter as they are taken from the oven. Cool on a wire rack.

DIRECTIONS FOR FREEZING BREADS

Breads can be frozen at several different points during the making and baking. I like to freeze rolls after they have risen the first time, shaped and sized, placed on a baking sheet and covered tightly with wax paper. They can then be thawed, allowed to double in size, and cooked as directed. Unless they are baked before thoroughly thawed, they will come out as fresh as if just made. When ready to use them, make sure to allow sufficient time for the correct thawing.

Loaf bread can be baked, completely cooled and then wrapped in foil or wax paper and frozen until time to use it. To serve it hot and as tasty as if just freshly baked, thaw completely, slice, butter it and form back into a loaf. Then wrap securely with foil and reheat in a 375° oven for about 20 minutes. Test to make sure all of the slices are hot before removing from the oven. Serve immediately. The loaf can be served without loss of texture, substance, or flavor.

YEAST BREAD ROLLS

Hot rolls that are served thoroughly cooked, brown, and with crisp crusts get more compliments from the audience than any other cooking endeavor.

Dinner rolls can be made from most of the yeast bread recipes in this book. However, I am giving some here which are a little lighter in texture and a little richer and which can be made in less time than those made from the regular loaf recipes.

Rolls have an advantage over many breads, in that they can be made into almost any shape or size and do not need to rise quite as long as loaf breads. They can be frozen with confidence. See directions for freezing.

Suggestions for shapes and sizes for dinner rolls and sweet breakfast rolls

PAN ROLLS

For quantity baking the pan roll is the most practical shape to make. To make these rolls form the dough into small balls, about 1 ounce each. Place them close together in a greased, shallow baking pan, or on baking sheets. They can be flattened slightly with the fingers before placing on the sheets. Cover and let rise until almost doubled. Brush with melted butter or margarine and bake at 400° for about 20 minutes, or until brown. For a very soft and tasty crust, brush them again with melted butter as they come from the oven.

PARKER HOUSE ROLLS

The name supposedly originated from a style of yeast roll made long ago in Boston at the Parker House boardinghouse. It was so light, delicious, and attractive that the name has been handed down to us. To make, roll out the dough to about 1/2-inch thick and with a biscuit cutter, cut rounds of about 2 inches in diameter. Dip each piece in melted butter, fold in half, or fold 1/3 of the round over, pressing the edges firmly together. Place them close together in a well-greased, shallow, baking pan. Cover and let rise for about 25 minutes. Brush again with melted butter and bake at 400° for about 20 minutes, or until brown. For a very rich, soft crust, brush again as they come from the oven.

CRESCENTS

To make these attractive rolls, roll a piece of dough into a circle about 12 inches in diameter, and about 1/4-inch thick. Cut into pie-shaped wedges. Brush each with melted butter if baking for dinner rolls. If making for sweet breakfast rolls that are to be filled with a sweet spread, see fillings p. 211 and follow directions. For dinner rolls, roll the wedge up slowly starting with the wide end. Place on greased baking sheets with the pointed end underneath. Cover and set to rise for about 30 minutes. When ready to bake, brush them with melted butter again, and bake in a preheated oven at 400° for about 15 minutes, or until brown. If they are being filled and served as a sweet roll, brush with a mixture of 1 beaten egg and 1 tablespoon warm water when ready to bake.

CLOVERLEAFS

Pinch off tiny balls from the dough and place 3 of these in each well-buttered muffin cup. Cover and let rise for about 20 minutes, or until almost doubled in bulk. Brush with melted butter or margarine, and bake at 400° for about 15 or 20 minutes, or until brown. Brush again with melted butter when removing from oven.

BUTTER FLUFFS or FAN TANS

Roll the dough to about 1/4-inch thickness in a long, oblong strip about 9 inches wide. Spread with melted butter and cut into 6 long strips, about 1 1/2 inches wide. Stack the 6 sticks evenly, one on top of the other. Cut this stack into 1-inch pieces. Place cut-side down in greased baking muffin cups. Cover and let rise for about 20 minutes. Brush with melted butter and bake at 400° for about 15 minutes or until brown.

YEAST BREAD ROLLS

To make about 3 dozen rolls, depending on shape and size

YOU WILL NEED
- 2 packages active dry yeast
- 1/2 cup lukewarm water
- 4 tablespoons sugar
- 1 3/4 cups milk
- 2 teaspoons salt
- 4 tablespoons shortening
- 2 eggs
- 6 to 6 1/2 cups all-purpose flour

THE PREPARATION

Scald the milk and while it is still hot add the shortening, sugar, and salt. Dissolve the yeast in the warm water and when the milk mixture has cooled to lukewarm, combine the two mixtures. Stir in the eggs and begin adding the flour, little by little. Beat either by hand or with an electric mixer. Keep adding the flour and beating until about 5 cups have been added. From then on add only enough to keep the dough manageable. The less flour used the lighter the roll. The dough should be firm, smooth, velvety, but soft.

Turn the dough into a deep, well-greased bowl, turn once to grease the top, cover, and set aside to rise until doubled in bulk, or a little more than doubled, about 1 1/2 hours.

When the dough has doubled, turn it out onto a floured surface, knead slightly, and divide into small portions for easy rolling and shaping. Roll out each portion to about 1/2-inch thick and cut to desired shape and size. (See directions for making sizes and shapes.) Place on a greased baking sheet, or in shallow baking pans, close together. Cover and let rise for about 30 minutes. (If they are to be frozen, cover them with wax paper and place in freezer at this point in the preparation.)

When they are ready to bake, brush them generously with melted butter or margarine, and bake in a preheated oven at 400° for about 15 minutes, or until brown. Brush again with melted butter when taking from oven. Serve at once. If circumstances demand that the rolls be kept warm for a time after baking, and if the church does not own a holding oven, wrap them securely in foil, and place in a warm oven (not hot) for a time.

WHOLE WHEAT ROLLS

To make about 3 dozen dinner rolls, depending on size and shape

YOU WILL NEED
- 2 packages active dry yeast
- 1/2 cup warm water
- 1 tablespoon salt
- 1/2 cup dark molasses
- 6 tablespoons shortening
- 1 1/2 cups milk
- 2 eggs
- 2 cups whole wheat flour, stone-ground
- 4 to 5 cups all-purpose flour
- butter or margarine for brushing

THE PREPARATION

Scald the milk and while it is still hot add the salt, molasses, and shortening. Dissolve the yeast in the warm water and when the milk mixture has cooled to lukewarm, combine the two mixtures. Stir in the eggs and start adding the flours. First add the whole wheat, beating in a little at a time, either by hand or with an electric mixer. After all the whole wheat has been added, start adding the all-purpose. When the dough becomes too thick to beat, add a little more of the all-purpose flour by mixing in with the hands. Rolls are lighter when a minimum of flour is used.

When the dough has reached a firm, but still soft stage, place in a deep, well-greased bowl, and turn once to grease the top. Cover and let rise until doubled in bulk, about 1 to 1 1/2 hours. When it has doubled, turn out onto a floured surface and knead slightly, adding a little flour if necessary to make handling easy. Divide the dough into small portions to make the rolling easy. Roll out each part to about 1/2-inch thickness, cut and shape according to needs. See suggestions for shaping. Then place on well-greased baking sheets, or in shallow baking pans, and cover to let rise again for about 30 minutes. Brush with melted butter and bake in a preheated oven at 400° for about 15 minutes or until brown. Brush again with melted butter as the rolls come from the oven.

SWEET YEAST BREADS AND ROLLS

This basic sweet yeast bread recipe can serve many purposes. It can be used for sweet rolls filled with a rich spread and served for breakfast, or it can be made into a beautiful round loaf with a dome. The domed loaf should have a glaze of a beaten egg mixture before baking. It is excellent served with butter and jam as a dessert.

The following recipe will make two large round loaves, or about 3 dozen breakfast sweet rolls (depending on size) which can be filled with jams, jellies, fruits, nuts, etc. To make a generous serving for 50 repeat this recipe once.

To make 2 large, round loaves, or about 3 dozen breakfast rolls

YOU WILL NEED
- 2 packages active dry yeast
- 1 cup lukewarm water
- 2 teaspoons salt
- 1 1/2 cups milk
- 3 eggs
- 3/4 cup sugar
- 3/4 cup sweet cream butter
- 6 to 7 1/2 cups all-purpose flour

THE PREPARATION

Scald the milk and, while it is still hot, add the sugar, butter, salt, and set aside to cool. Dissolve the yeast in the warm water and, when the milk mixture has cooled to lukewarm, combine the two mixtures. Beat in the eggs and start adding the flour little by little, beating either by hand or with an electric mixer. After the batter has absorbed as much of the flour as can be beaten in, add a little more by mixing with the hands. The dough will be quite rich, a bit sticky, but should be firm enough to handle, although still soft. Form it into a ball, set in a deep, greased bowl, cover with wax paper, and refrigerate for several hours or overnight. If time demands using it at once, cover with a cloth, place in a warm spot (not hot) and let rise until doubled in bulk, about 1 1/2 hours.

If the dough has been refrigerated, which is the better way to make it, it may fall after having been doubled for sometime. That will not matter, just punch it down, knead it slightly, and proceed with the preparation.

When it has doubled in bulk, turn it out onto a floured surface and divide into two equal parts. If making round loaves, pinch off a part of each for the dome, and form the large part into a round loaf or loaves. Place them in well-greased round pans, about 3 or 4 inches in depth, and make a small ball of the pinched off part. Set this small amount in the center of each round. Cover the loaves and set aside to rise until doubled in bulk, about 45 minutes. When ready to bake, brush the loaves with a mixture of 1 beaten egg and 1 tablespoon warm water. Bake in a preheated oven at 350° for about 40 minutes, or until the bread is brown and pulled from the sides of the pans. It should sound hollow when thumped with the fingers if it is done. Cool on a wire rack.

If sweet rolls are being made with this dough follow the directions given for shapes, sizes, and fillings. See pp. 68ff.

Suggested Fillings for Sweet Rolls

The average amount of filling for each roll depends largely on its size and shape. If the sweet roll is a medium size, 1 to 1 1/2 tablespoons of filling will make a spread sufficient to give it a full flavor. A cup of filling usually makes enough to spread 8 to 10 rolls. To find the right proportion for the combinations suggested, make 1 cup at a time until the desired amount can be determined. The cook should also decide on which flavor to emphasize when putting these combinations together. In other words, experiment.

Some combinations:

1. 1 egg yolk, beaten
   1 teaspoon grated orange rind
   3 tablespoons lemon juice
   1/2 cup sugar
   1/3 cup soft bread crumbs, or enough to make a spreading mixture

2. 1/2 cup sweetened applesauce
   1/2 cup ground raisins
   1/8 teaspoon cinnamon
   1/4 cup heavy cream, or sufficient to make the mixture spread

3. 1/3 cup finely chopped almonds
   1/3 cup apricot jam
   heavy cream or melted butter to make a spread

4. 1 tablespoon grated orange rind
1/2 cup sugar
1/2 cup bread crumbs
1/2 cup finely chopped nuts
melted butter to make the mixture spread

NORWEGIAN COFFEE CAKE

This is a gooey, rich, yeast cake or bread, which can be served as a dessert or as a breakfast sweet bread.

To make approximately 25 servings

YOU WILL NEED

3/4 cup cottage cheese, sieved
1 package active dry yeast
1/3 cup lukewarm water
3 eggs
1/2 cup sugar
1/2 cup soft butter
2 teaspoons salt
1/2 teaspoon soda
1 tablespoon grated lemon rind
1 cup strawberry preserves (or other fruit preserves or jam)
3 to 4 cups all-purpose flour

The glaze:
1 beaten egg
1 tablespoon warm water

THE PREPARATION

Prepare the cheese by pressing it through a sieve, or put through a blender. It should be smooth and creamy. Dissolve the yeast in the warm water, and in a large mixing bowl combine all of the ingredients except the flour and preserves. Stir or beat the mixture until smooth. Add the flour little by little, beating either by hand or with electric mixer. When the dough becomes too thick to beat, add a little more flour by mixing with the hands. The dough should be soft but firm enough to handle. Place in a deep, well-greased bowl, cover, and let rise until doubled in bulk, about 1 hour or a little longer.

After the dough has doubled in bulk, turn it out onto a floured surface and knead slightly. Roll out to an oblong about 1/2 inch thick and about 16 inches long and 20 inches wide. Place the dough in a well-greased baking pan, about 10 x 15 inches, or a little bigger. Place the dough in such a manner that the wide sides will hang over the edges in order to be folded back over the preserves. Spread the bottom part of the dough with melted butter then a layer of the preserves over the butter. Pull the sides hanging over the edges back to touch in the center. With a sharp, pointed knife make small diagonal slashes in the dough on both sides of the center. The mass should resemble a blanket with preserves peeking through down the center and through the slashes. Spread the top with the beaten egg and 1 tablespoon warm water mixture. Cover and set aside to rise for about 20 minutes. Bake in a preheated oven at 375° for about 30 minutes or until brown. The preserves will ooze out and make a rich, sweet cake or bread. Slice in whatever size desired. Serve hot or cold.

QUICK BREADS

Breads made with leavening other than yeast are called quick breads because they contain a leavening agent that acts quickly. This type of bread includes biscuits, muffins, corn breads, pan breads, griddle cakes, coffee cakes, sweet dessert breads, and others that are made with baking powder, soda, or eggs as leavening agents.

BAKING POWDER BISCUITS

When making biscuits the ingredients should be handled as little and as quickly as possible. To make a light, tender biscuit handle it just enough to gather the ingredients together, then shape and bake. To serve 50 people, prepare at least 2 biscuits for each. Biscuits can be frozen after they are placed on the baking sheet, later thawed, and baked according to directions.

To make approximately 100 biscuits

YOU WILL NEED
- 20 cups all-purpose flour
- 2 tablespoons salt
- 2 cups vegetable shortening
- 1/2 cup baking powder
- 2 quarts milk, approximately

THE PREPARATION

Sift the flour, salt, and baking powder together into a large bowl. Work the shortening either with a pastry blender or with the fingers into the flour mixture until it resembles cornmeal. Add the milk slowly, pulling the mixture together into a soft ball. Use only the amount of milk necessary to accomplish this. Divide the roll into three or four parts to make the rolling easy. Roll or pat out the parts to about 1/2-inch thickness. Cut the dough with a biscuit cutter to the desired size, and place on greased baking sheets. Brush the tops with milk or with melted butter, and bake in a preheated oven at 425° for about 15 minutes, or until brown. Biscuits can be refrigerated after they are placed on a baking sheet and baked when needed, without loss of lightness or texture.

VARIATIONS

Cheese biscuits. Reduce the shortening by 1/2 cup and add 1 pound grated sharp cheese to the flour before the milk is added.

Sage biscuits. Add 3 tablespoons of rubbed sage to the flour after it has been sifted with the other dry ingredients.

Whole wheat biscuits. Substitute 2 1/2 cups of whole wheat flour for the same amount of all-purpose.

Sausage biscuits. Reduce the shortening by 1/2 cup and add 3/4 cup finely crumbled, cooked, and highly seasoned sausage to the dough while it is being pulled together.

BUTTERMILK BISCUITS

To make approximately 100 biscuits

YOU WILL NEED
20 cups all-purpose flour
3 tablespoons salt
4 tablespoons baking powder
3 teaspoons soda
2 quarts buttermilk, approximately
2 cups shortening

THE PREPARATION

Follow the directions given for making baking powder biscuits.

VARIATIONS

Bacon biscuits. Reduce the shortening by 1/4 cup and add 1 cup fried, crisp, crumbled bacon to the dough, then bake as directed.

Mexican Chili biscuits. Reduce the flour by 2 cups, substitute 2 cups yellow cornmeal, add 2 tablespoon chili powder and 1/2 teaspoon cumin powder. Serve with a pot of red beans which have been cooked with ground meat.

PLAIN MUFFINS
a basic recipe

A package of muffin ready-mix is often used nowadays; however, for those who like the old-fashioned method of making them from the beginning to the end, I am giving this recipe with some variations. The do-it-our-way muffin has a fuller and more lasting flavor.

To make approximately 5 dozen muffins depending on size

YOU WILL NEED
- 9 cups all-purpose flour
- 1 cup sugar, or 1 1/2 cups honey
- 1 tablespoon salt
- 6 eggs, beaten
- 4 tablespoons baking powder
- 1 cup melted margarine
- 2 quarts milk, approximately

THE PREPARATION

Cream the sugar and margarine, and stir in the beaten eggs. Sift the salt, baking powder, and flour together and combine the two mixtures alternately with the milk. Use just enough milk to make a thick batter, but thin enough to spoon easily. Spoon into well-greased muffin tins, to about 2/3 full. Bake in a preheated oven at 400° for about 15 minutes or until brown.

VARIATIONS

Orange Marmalade muffins. Place a teaspoon of marmalade on the top of each muffin just before baking. Or use some other jam, jelly, or preserves instead.

Pecan muffins. Add 2 cups finely chopped pecan meats to the batter just before spooning into muffin pans.

Raisin muffins. Add 2 cups of raisins, which have been dusted with flour, to the batter just before spooning into the muffin tins.

CORN BREADS

One of the most important facts of American food history is that corn was introduced to us by the Indians. For that we are eternally grateful. It has become one of the staples of our best foods. Cornmeal gives bread a crumbly texture and a slight sweetness. There are many varieties of corn bread, but I am giving only three in this book. The imaginative cook can add her version to any of these three and come up with a delicious addition to a menu.

BUTTERMILK CORNBREAD

To make approximately 50 servings

YOU WILL NEED
- 2 quarts, plus 1 cup, cornmeal, white or yellow
- 1 1/2 cups all-purpose flour
- 4 tablespoons baking powder
- 2 1/2 teaspoons soda
- 2 1/2 tablespoons salt
- 10 eggs, beaten
- 1 cup bacon fat, or margarine, melted
- 2 quarts buttermilk, approximately

THE PREPARATION

In a large bowl combine all dry ingredients and stir until well blended. Add beaten eggs and melted fat and stir well. Add the buttermilk a little at a time and keep adding until the batter is thick, but still thin enough to pour. Pour into well-greased, preheated, baking pans. The grease in the pans should be hot but not smoking. If possible use heavy skillets or iron corn pans for the baking. Bake at 400° for about 25 minutes, or until brown and pulled from the sides of the pans.

SPOON BREAD
Deep South

According to legend, spoon bread had its beginning in the Deep South. It was first made so much like a custard that it had to be eaten with a spoon, thus the name. If the following recipe comes out so soft that it needs to be eaten with a spoon, perhaps that is because it is authentic.

To make 25 generous servings

YOU WILL NEED
- 2 quarts boiling water
- 1 quart yellow cornmeal
- 1 quart milk
- 2 1/2 tablespoons salt
- 4 tablespoons baking powder
- 1 cup soft butter or margarine
- 12 eggs, beaten

THE PREPARATION

Pour the boiling water over the cornmeal and stir until smooth. Add the milk, salt, beaten eggs, baking powder, and butter, and stir or beat until blended. Pour the mixture into a hot, buttered baking pan, or pans, and bake in a preheated oven at 400° for about 25 minutes, or until the center of the batter springs back when touched with the fingers. The center should be well set when the bread is done. The finished bread is almost custardlike, quite soft but completely cooked. It can be served with any meal, or eaten with sweet syrups or honey at any time. Delicious.

SPOON BREAD
Mexican-Style

If you see a recipe for this bread that does not include some type of a green or hot chili pepper, you will know that it did not come from the Southwest. Chili, whether hot, green, red, or mild is one of the most widely used seasonings of Mexican cookery. The finished product of this recipe may be soft, but it should be firm enough to cut when serving. The pieces should be small if the crowd is not accustomed to bold seasonings.

To make approximately 50 servings

YOU WILL NEED
- 2 No. 3 cans (about 8 cups) cream-style corn
- 2 quarts milk
- 2 quarts yellow cornmeal, about 2 pounds
- 12 eggs, beaten
- 1 1/2 tablespoons salt
- 1 teaspoon soda
- 3 tablespoons baking powder
- 1 cup margarine or bacon fat
- 2 cups canned hot green chili peppers, fine chopped (4 4-ounce cans)
- 1 1/2 pounds grated sharp cheese

THE PREPARATION

In a large bowl stir the cornmeal, soda, baking powder, and salt together until blended. Add all other ingredients, except the chilis and cheese. Pour one-half of this mixture into well-greased baking pans, spread evenly. Over this mixture sprinkle half of the chopped chilis and half of the cheese. Pour the remainder of the mixture over this and then sprinkle the remainder of chilis and cheese over top of all. The first chili-cheese mixture may come to the top as the bread bakes, but that is the manner of this dish. Bake in a preheated oven at 400° for about 35 minutes, or until the bread is brown and well set. Test for doneness by pressing the finger in the center of the bread; if it springs back, it is done.

NUT BREAD
a basic recipe

This bread can be made long in advance, frozen, and thawed to room temperature before serving without loss of flavor or texture.

To make approximately 5 loaves, 4 x 9-inches (serving 12 to 14 slices each)

YOU WILL NEED
12 cups all-purpose flour
2 tablespoons baking powder
3 cups nuts, pecans or walnuts
3/4 cup melted butter or margarine
3 cups sugar
2 teaspoons salt
6 eggs, beaten
6 cups milk

THE PREPARATION

Combine all of the dry ingredients in a large bowl, and stir until well blended. Add the eggs, milk, melted shortening and beat or stir until smooth. Fold in the nuts and pour into 5 (4 x 9) well-greased and floured loaf pans. Bake in a preheated oven at 375° for about 1 hour, or until the bread pulls from the sides of the pans and springs back when pressed with the fingers. Remove from pans and cool on a wire rack.

VARIATIONS

Banana nut bread. Reduce the flour by 1 cup and add 3 cups mashed ripe bananas and 1/2 teaspoon soda. Bake as directed for nut bread.
Applesauce nut bread. Add 3 cups applesauce, well-seasoned with sugar and spices, & 1 teaspoon soda. If the batter appears too thin, add about 1/2 cup flour to thicken.

ORANGE-RAISIN BREAD

Four medium loaves, each cutting about 14 slices, make sufficient to serve 50 people.

To make 4 medium loaves

YOU WILL NEED

3 cups sugar
1 cup margarine or butter
1 teaspoon salt
8 eggs
3 tablespoons baking powder
1 1/2 teaspoons soda
8 cups all-purpose flour
2 cups orange juice
3 cups *ground* raisins
4 tablespoons grated orange rind

The glaze:
2 cups orange juice
4 cups sugar

THE PREPARATION

In a large bowl cream the sugar, butter, and eggs together until well blended. Reserve a little flour to dust the raisins, and sift the remainder with baking powder, salt, and soda. Combine the two mixtures and beat in the orange juice and rind. Fold in the ground raisins, which have been dusted with some of the flour. Pour into well-greased and floured loaf pans and bake in a preheated oven at 350° for about 40 minutes, or until the loaves test done. Prepare the glaze while the loaves are baking. As they come from the oven and are turned out to cool, right side-up, dribble the glaze mixture over them. Allow the glaze to penetrate the loaves as much as possible while it is being added. A delicious dessert or a breakfast feast.

> When work seems rather dull to us
> And life is not so sweet,
> One thing at least brings joy;
> We all simply love to eat.
> —H. Best

CARROT BREAD

To make approximately 25 servings

YOU WILL NEED

2 cups grated fresh carrots
3 eggs
1/3 cup salad oil
1/2 teaspoon salt
3/4 cup sugar
1 tablespoon cocoa, and 1 teaspoon instant coffee crystals dissolved in 1/3 cup boiling water
1 tablespoon grated orange rind
2 teaspoons soda
1 teaspoon baking powder
1/2 cup whole wheat flour
2 1/2 cups all-purpose flour
3/4 cup finely chopped nuts

THE PREPARATION

Dissolve the cocoa and instant coffee crystals in the boiling water and set aside. Sift the flour, salt, soda, and baking powder together and stir into this mixture the oil, sugar, carrots, orange rind, eggs, and cocoa mixture. Beat until blended. Fold in the nuts and pour into two small loaf pans, well-greased and floured. Or bake in one pan about 10 x 10 inches, or use whatever size is suitable for the occasion. Bake in a preheated oven at 350° for about 45 minutes or until the bread pulls from the sides of the pans and springs back when touched in the center with the fingers. It should be very moist and tasty.

CREOLE DOUGHNUTS
(Beignets)

These yeast square doughnuts are fabulous for a party, since their shape and lightness make them perfect for the "dunkin' " fun. A cup of New Orleans coffee served with square doughnuts adds interest to any gathering, whether it is a party or a church supper.

To serve 50 people generously make this recipe twice.

To make about 5 dozen, average size doughnuts

YOU WILL NEED
- 1 cup boiling water
- 4 tablespoons shortening
- 1/2 cup sugar
- 1 teaspoon salt
- 1 cup evaporated milk
- 1 package dry yeast
- 1/2 cup warm water
- 2 eggs, beaten
- 7 1/2 cups all-purpose flour, approximately
- fat for frying
- powdered sugar

THE PREPARATION

Pour the boiling water over the shortening, sugar, and salt. Add the milk and let stand until the mixture cools to lukewarm. Dissolve the yeast in the warm water and add to milk mixture. Stir in the beaten eggs. Stir in 4 cups of the flour and beat well. Add enough more flour to make a soft dough. Place in a greased bowl, grease the top and cover with wax paper and a cloth. Refrigerate for an hour or more.

When ready to make the doughnuts, divide the dough into small parts. Roll each part out to about 1/4-inch thickness. Cut into small squares, about 2 x 2 inches and fry, a few at a time, in deep, hot fat. Make a test of the fat by dropping a small piece of dough in to see if the fat is hot enough. Do not let the dough rise before frying. The squares should brown on one side, then be turned to brown on the other. Drain on absorbent paper. Sprinkle with powdered sugar.

A PIZZA FOR A PARTY

When the church supper is for the young people, do them a big favor and make enough of these pizzas to fill them up—that could take a bit of cooking!

To make 4 large pizzas, serving 6 to 8 wedges each

YOU WILL NEED
- 2 cups lukewarm water
- 2 packages active dry yeast
- 2 teaspoons sugar
- 1 tablespoon salt
- 2 tablespoons melted shortening
- 6 cups all-purpose flour approximately

THE PREPARATION

Dissolve the yeast with the sugar in the lukewarm water, then add the salt, melted shortening, and 1 cup of the flour. Beat until smooth. Keep adding the flour little by little, stirring or beating until the dough is quite firm but not sticky. Cover and set aside to rest for 20 minutes. Divide the dough into 4 equal parts, and on a floured surface knead each slightly, and form into a ball. Flatten the ball by rolling, patting, pulling, and stretching gently. (Try not to break the dough.) Stretch the dough to fit the bottom of 4 round pizza pans, 12 inches in diameter. Grease the pans and fit the stretched dough into the bottom of the pans, pressing about 1-inch around the outer edge to form a rim. Cover and let rise for about 20 minutes. While the dough is rising prepare whatever spread is to be used for the top. When it is ready to bake, brush with salad oil and spread the prepared mixture well over the top. Bake in a preheated oven at 425° for about 30 minutes or until the edges of the crust are brown and the spread appears well cooked.

Suggestions for combinations of spreads for the pizzas

1. A mixture of canned tomato pureé with grated sharp cheese, 1 tablespoon grated onion, some finely diced sausages, and a generous sprinkle of oregano. It takes about 1 cup or a little more of this mixture to spread over a 12-inch pizza.

2. A mixture of chopped fresh green peppers, diced fresh tomatoes, grated sharp cheese, diced ham, with a sprinkle of oregano. It takes about 1 cup, or a little more, of this mixture for each 12-inch pizza.

CREAM PUFFS

To serve these as a dessert use a pastry tube to form them on the baking sheet and when they are baked split them, and fill with a cream custard, topped with a chocolate frosting. If they are to be served as an entreé, or as a part of the entreé, place the batter on the baking sheet with a large spoon. When they are baked, cut off the very top and fill with a chicken salad, creamed chicken, shrimp or crab salad, etc.

To make about 50 large or 100 small puffs

YOU WILL NEED
- 1 quart boiling water
- 1 pound margarine or butter
- 4 1/2 cups all-purpose flour
- 2 1/2 teaspoons salt
- 16 large or 18 medium eggs

THE PREPARATION

Bring the water to a full boil and add the margarine, salt, and flour all at once. Beat vigorously. When the mixture leaves the sides of the kettle, which it soon will, transfer to a bowl that can be used for mixing. Cool for a few minutes, then start adding the eggs. Add one at a time and beat well after each addition. Continue adding and beating until all are added. Drop the batter on a greased baking sheet, either with a pastry tube or with a large spoon. If with a pastry tube, place in strips, about 4 1/2 inches in length. Bake in a preheated oven at 425° for about 15 minutes, then reduce the heat to 325° and continue baking for another 30 minutes. Make a test of one before removing all from oven. Take one out; if it collapses, it needs more baking.

CHEESE BALLS

These can be made and frozen, thawed and used as needed, or they can be reheated to serve hot with salads and soups or eaten with an entreé. Also, they can be made into different shapes and sizes to go with a party relish platter. Pile them high in the center of a round tray of colorful relishes for something special.

To make about 4 dozen small balls

YOU WILL NEED
- 2 5-ounce jars of sharp cheese spread
- 6 tablespoons melted butter
- 1 1/2 cups all-purpose flour
- 1 teaspoon salt
- 1/2 teaspoon paprika
- 1/8 teaspoon cayenne pepper, more or less

THE PREPARATION

Blend all the ingredients together well. Pinch off a small amount at a time, roll into a ball about 1 inch in diameter. Lay the balls on trays and refrigerate for about 2 hours. This helps keep them intact as they are baking. Place on ungreased baking sheets and bake at 400° for 10 to 15 minutes, or until slightly brown. Adjust the seasonings to suit the taste. Serve hot or cold.

CHEESE WAFERS

My dear friend, Lilita McCorkle, gave me this recipe with a generous sample years ago. I have made them dozens of times since and have shared her recipe with others. These are excellent served with a plate of relishes or with other appetizers.

To make approximately 8 dozen, 1 1/2-inch rounds (or squares)

YOU WILL NEED
- 2 cups butter or margarine
- 4 cups flour
- 8 cups grated sharp cheese (about 2 pounds)
- 4 cups finely chopped nuts
- 4 teaspoons salt
- 1 teaspoon cayenne pepper, more or less

THE PREPARATION

Cream all of the ingredients together until the mixture forms a sticky ball. (I use my hands to do the mixing.) Form into rolls about 1 1/2 inches in diameter (or make a square form). Place in refrigerator for several hours or overnight (or freeze). When ready to make, grease a cookie sheet slightly, slice the roll thin and bake until light brown at 325° for about 15 minutes.

SOUPS

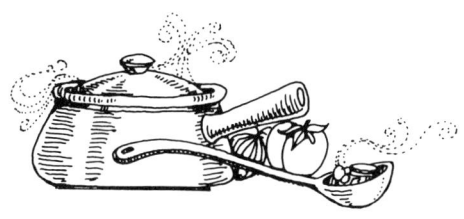

Soups made from scratch should play an important part when preparing the menus for church suppers. A delicious, nourishing, and economical meal of soup can be made for a large crowd with a great variety of ingredients. Making soup offers more opportunities for the cooks to experiment than almost any other item on the menu.

For 50 servings, to adults, of soups for a first course, make about 2 1/2 gallons. This will make 1/2 cup to 2/3 cup for each serving. For the main course, or when the soup is a one-meal dish, make about 3 gallons, which will serve each of 50 people 1 cup or more.

CREAM OF POTATO SOUP

To make 50 generous servings

YOU WILL NEED

2 gallons water
4 tablespoons salt
1 teaspoon black pepper
10 pounds potatoes, peeled and sliced
1 cup finely chopped onions
1 pound breakfast bacon, chopped
1/2 cup butter or margarine
1/2 cup flour
5 quarts milk

THE PREPARATION

Add salt to the 2 gallons of water and bring to a boil. Add the peeled and sliced potatoes, pepper, onions, and bacon and cook until all ingredients are tender, about 20 minutes. With a potato masher press all the ingredients into a mushlike mass and set the whole aside. Taste for seasonings and correct if necessary. Melt the butter, stir in the flour, and cook for about 5 minutes. Add the milk to the mixture slowly to make a thin sauce, stir until smooth, cook for about 10 minutes. Combine the two mixtures and strain. Force the ingredients through the strainer to capture the substance of the soup and to help thicken it. Reheat slowly and serve hot.

CREAM OF CORN SOUP

For a soup-and-salad supper you will find this soup excellent for the heavy part of the meal. A tasty salad of fruits and cheeses, plus toasted French bread should make a church supper super.

To make 25 generous servings

YOU WILL NEED
one No. 10 can of corn, cream-style
1 quart milk
1 quart chicken broth
1 quart water
1/2 cup finely chopped onion
1/2 cup flour
1/2 cup butter
salt
black pepper
2 cups thinly sliced potatoes

THE PREPARATION

Bring the water and chicken broth to a boil and add 2 teaspoons salt, 1 teaspoon black pepper, the corn, and onion. (The broth will be salty already, therefore, salt with caution.) Reduce the heat and cook slowly for about 10 minutes or until the onion is tender. Taste for seasoning. Heat the milk in a separate saucepan until almost boiling, but do not boil. Add this to the first mixture, slowly. Stir in the potatoes, which have been peeled and sliced, and return to heat. Simmer just until the potatoes are tender, about 15 minutes. Melt the butter in a saucepan and stir in the flour. Cook over low heat for about 5 minutes. Dip 3 or 4 cups of the soup into the butter mixture and stir until smooth. Combine the mixtures and stir until blended. Press the soup through a strainer with a wooden spoon to make it smooth and to extract all of the substance possible. Return to the heat and keep hot until it is served. It should be the consistency of a thick cream, but it will be delicious whether thick or thin.

CREAM OF TOMATO SOUP

A hot tomato soup served on a cold night with a roast beef dinner is something to delight the most discriminating appetite. In addition to the soup and roast beef, a fruit salad with hot muffins and chocolate custard for dessert would complete an elegant menu.

To make approximately 50 servings of 1 cup each

YOU WILL NEED
- 2 No. 10 cans tomato juice, or 6 1/2 quarts
- 1 cup sliced onions
- 3 bay leaves
- 1 teaspoon soda
- 1 cup margarine
- 1/2 cup sugar
- 2 1/2 tablespoons salt, more or less
- 1 tablespoon black pepper
- 1/2 cup flour
- 6 quarts milk, hot

THE PREPARATION

Add the onions and bay leaves to the tomato juice and bring to a boil. Simmer until the onion is tender, about 15 minutes. Add the soda, which helps prevent curdling. Add the sugar, salt, and pepper and remove from the heat. Remove the bay leaves. Melt the margarine and stir in the flour. Heat the milk to hot but do not boil, and gradually add to the butter mixture, stirring and adding slowly until well blended. Combine the mixtures, which should be hot when combining. Strain and serve while still very hot. If the mixture should separate—it often does—while preparing, it can be beaten smooth again.

RED BEAN SOUP

The red bean, the pinto, or the Mexican frijoles may be used in this recipe without change of amounts. I often make this soup with the pinto bean, which is quite popular in the South and Southwest, and use bold and daring seasonings.

To make 50 generous servings

YOU WILL NEED

4 1/2 pounds red beans
4 gallons, or more, water
2 pounds salt pork, sliced
1 1/2 cups chopped onions
3 tablespoons salt
1/2 teaspoon cayenne pepper
4 tablespoons chili powder (optional)

THE PREPARATION

Bring the water to a boil and add the salt, salt pork, onions, and beans which have been thoroughly washed and soaked ahead for several hours. Boil the mixture slowly for 3 or 4 hours, until the beans are quite tender. The beans should be kept covered with boiling water at all times while they are cooking. After they are tender, taste for salt, since the salt pork will have added salt, the seasonings may need correcting. Add the cayenne pepper a little at a time, and taste for amount desired. Add the chili powder, if using, and remove the salt pork before serving. Serve hot. Try serving cornbread with this soup.

VARIATION

For a Mexican bean soup. Add more water to the soup about 1 hour before taking from the fire, and add 4 pounds of well-seasoned ground beef. Add 1 cup finely diced green chilis if a highly seasoned soup is in order.

SPLIT-PEA SOUP

To make approximately 50 generous servings

YOU WILL NEED

3 1/2 pounds split peas
2 1/2 gallons water
salt
1 large ham bone
1 1/2 pounds sliced salt pork
1 cup finely chopped onions
1 tablespoon white pepper
1/3 cup lemon juice
2 quarts thin white sauce
pimiento strips for garnish

THE PREPARATION

Wash the peas thoroughly and set aside. Bring the water to a boil, add the ham bone and salt pork. When the meats have boiled enough to flavor the liquid, add the onions, pepper, and lemon juice. The lemon juice will give a spark of tartness to an otherwise flat pea flavor. Add the peas and cook slowly until the peas are completely tender and disintegrated, about 2 hours. Remove the ham bone and strain the mixture. Set aside. Salt only after tasting, since the salt pork and ham bone may have added sufficient salt. Make 2 quarts of thin white sauce according to directions. See p. 126. Combine the two mixtures and reheat over low fire. If the soup becomes too thick, thin with a little hot milk. Serve while very hot. For a garnish place a strip of pimiento in the center of each bowl of soup to add a bit of glamour to an otherwise colorless dish.

FRENCH ONION SOUP with Cheese

To make approximately 50 servings

YOU WILL NEED

2 gallons canned beef broth or consommé
3 quarts sliced onion rings
1 pound margarine
3/4 cup all-purpose flour
1/2 cup Worcestershire sauce
1/4 teaspoon cayenne pepper
3 tablespoons paprika
salt, if needed

For top:
1 1/2 pounds grated sharp cheese

THE PREPARATION

Grate the cheese and set aside. In a large heavy kettle, melt the margarine and sauté the onions. Stir and turn them as they cook to prevent burning. As soon as they are slightly brown, add the flour and toss and stir until well blended. Add paprika, cayenne pepper, and the Worcestershire sauce. Set aside. Bring the broth to a boil, but do not boil, and combine the two mixtures. The broth will be salty, but taste for any extra salt that might be needed. Simmer for about 20 minutes, and serve very hot with a tablespoon of grated cheese in the center of each bowl.

A SOUP FROM LEFTOVERS

When you have sufficient leftovers, make a soup. You can use meats, vegetables, casseroles, vegetable salads, or a combination of some of these. Freeze them immediately after the meal, well marked as to content and date. When you have accumulated 3 or 4 quarts, you are ready to make a soup.

They that have no other meat,
Bread and butter are glad to eat.
—John Clarke

To make approximately 50 servings from leftovers

YOU WILL NEED
3 or 4 quarts, or more, of frozen leftovers
2 gallons beef or chicken broth
seasonings, see herbs

THE PREPARATION

Bring the broth to a boil and dump in the frozen leftovers. Reduce the heat and simmer until all the mixture is well blended and all separate ingredients quite tender. Add whatever seasonings are in order. Taste before adding salt. Strain the mixture, forcing the ingredients through the strainer, to regain as much of the substance and the flavors as possible. Reheat and serve hot. If the color of the soup is a little blah—add a teaspoon of minced green pepper to the center of each bowl before serving.

CORN AND CHICKEN CHOWDER

The main difference between a chowder and a regular soup is that the chowder has chunks of meat left in it rather than just the essence of the meat blended into the liquid. It is a heavy, thick soup served most often as the main course. Recipes for chowder usually include bacon and salt pork in addition to bits of some other kind of meat.

To make approximately 50 servings

YOU WILL NEED
1 No. 10 can whole-kernel corn
1 pound salt pork, sliced
1 pound breakfast bacon, sliced
1/2 cup flour
4 to 5 pounds of chicken, cooked, boned, and cubed
1 cup sliced onions
2 gallons milk, hot
2 tablespoons salt
2 pounds potatoes, cooked and diced

THE PREPARATION

Prepare the chicken ahead and set aside. In a large heavy kettle fry the salt pork, bacon, and onion until the onions are tender and the pork and bacon almost crisp. Remove the pork, onions, and bacon from the fat. Set aside. Stir the flour into the fat left from the meats and cook for 2 or 3 minutes. Gradually add the hot milk to the flour mixture, stirring constantly to keep smooth, until all milk has been added. Add the potatoes and salt if needed. Taste for correct seasonings. The pork and bacon will have been salty, therefore salt with caution. Fold in the chicken, corn, onions, pork, and bacon and simmer over low heat for about 20 minutes, stirring carefully to keep all ingredients intact. Serve hot.

RELISHES AND GARNISHES

A touch of some colorful vegetable, fruit, or a combination of one or more of these, not only can add appetizing appeal but can be a perfect beginning or an enhancing ending to a meal. All vegetable relishes and garnishes should be fresh and crisp, and (usually) served cold. There are of course, a few exceptions.

The following suggestions are given as helps for the cooks who will think of many more to add to the list:

Carrot curls. Cut long, narrow, paper-thin slices and roll the strip around the finger. Fasten with a toothpick and chill in ice water for several hours. Remove the toothpick, shake off the water. Use as a part of a relish dish, or serve as a garnish for salads and meats.

Celery curls. Cut celery into 2 1/2-inch lengths. Cut each length into narrow paper-thin strips. Place in ice water for several hours. These should form rings or curls.

Cauliflower. Remove or separate the flowerlets from the cauliflower head into tiny ones. Marinate these in oil and vinegar dressing and chill. Arrange on a relish tray in design with green peppers and strips of pimiento.

Cucumbers. Cut into thin strips, or slice. Marinate in oil and vinegar dressing. Or stuff with yellow cheese, after removing seeds, and then slice into thin rings. Use an assortment of pickles, sweet, sour, dill, or mustard pickles.

Green peppers. Slice into rings, chill and lay in design with pieces of pimiento. Slice in thin rings and fill center with sieved hard-cooked egg yolk, or a combination of hard-cooked egg whites and yolk.

Lettuce. Use endive, bibb, garden variety, romaine, head lettuce, etc. Serve shredded or in wedges, as a base for salads or as a relish.

Grapes. Use in small bunches, glazed, or divide the bunch and use to stuff fruit halves, pears and peaches, etc. Serve white, purple, or red grapes on the relish tray fresh and chilled.

Olives. Stuffed green, ripe or sliced olives may be placed in design on cheese molds.

Radishes. Make them resemble roses, with a petallike shape. Cut off the root end with a sharp knife. Leave an inch or two of the green stem, then cut 4 or 5 petal-shaped slices around the radish from cut tip to center. Chill in ice water until petals spring open.

Some suggested foods to use as garnishes

Cheese. Balls, small or large; grated cheese; shaped and designed by pressing through a pastry tube, after making soft with sour cream, cream cheese, or milk; cheese straws.

Eggs. Hard-cooked, sliced, chopped, sieved.

Fruits. Watermelon and cantaloupe balls; lemon and orange slices and sections; grapefruit sections; peach and pear halves filled with jams or jellies; spiced peaches, whole, served with meats; cherries, candied or fresh or canned, well drained; apple rings; mint jelly; cranberries, fresh or jellied and cut into shapes; grapes, all colors.

Vegetables. See relishes also. Beets, pickled cut into designs; red cabbage, shredded, served with salads or with meats; peppers, green and red, cut into rings and placed in design over cheese molds, meats or salads; pimiento strips; tomato wedges and asparagus tips placed on meat slices.

Miscellaneous. Shredded chocolate over puddings, ice creams, and other desserts; nuts of all kinds—almonds, walnuts, pecans, etc.; prunes stuffed with cream cheese; tiny squares of toasted breads.

SALADS

Salads will always be one of the main and most important divisions of a well-balanced meal. A small plate of crisp, cold vegetables with a tart dressing, or a plate of colorful fruits with a base of shredded lettuce, gives the meal that certain zest and appeal that no other food or combination of foods can give.

The salad should supplement the main dish or add balance to the total meal, but never compete with the entreé or duplicate any other part of the menu.

Fresh fruits and melons. These are bulk salads and the average serving, for adults, is from 1/3 cup to 2/3 cup, depending on the water content of the fruit. When the occasion demands that a fruit salad be stretched at the last minute, crisp shredded lettuce can be added. Fruits and melon for salads should be prepared an hour or two ahead, and chilled before combining with the dressing. Melon and fruit combination salads are especially elegant in a watermelon half which has been scooped out. This combination is beautiful served on a bed of shredded lettuce on a large platter. Individual servings are always in order.

For fresh fruits and melon salads or combinations of these salads, I suggest the following dressings: (see recipes pp. 104)
1. Poppy seed dressing, 1 1/2 quarts for 50 servings
2. Celery seed dressing, 1 1/2 quarts for 50 servings
3. Sesame seed dressing, 1 1/2 quarts for 50 servings
4. 2 cups heavy cream, whipped and folded into any one of above
5. 2 cups sour cream, whipped and folded into any one of the above

The following suggestions are given for portions, measurements, and combinations of fruits and melon salads. These combinations can be altered to fit the fruits available. To make a generous 1/2-cup serving for 50 people you will need a total of 8 to 10 quarts of the salad.

1. **Strawberry & Avocado**
    5 quarts fresh ripe strawberries, some stemmed and sliced, some whole
    2 quarts avocados, peeled and sliced and sprinkled with lemon juice
    2 quarts orange sections
    1 1/2 quarts poppy seed dressing
2. **Papaya and Avocado**
    4 quarts papayas, peeled, seeded, and sliced
    4 quarts avocados, peeled and sliced
    1 1/2 quarts poppy seed dressing
3. **Honeydew Melon with Strawberries**
    4 quarts Honeydew melon, peeled and diced
    6 quarts strawberries, stemmed and whole
    Poppy seed dressing with whipped cream
4. **Melon-Melon**
    4 quarts watermelon, peeled and chunked
    2 quarts honeydew melon, peeled and chunked
    3 quarts cantaloupe, peeled and chunked
    Melon halves, hollowed out for bowls—optional
    Poppy seed dressing or sesame seed dressing

5. Grapes with Fruits
   2 quarts white seedless grapes
   3 quarts pineapple chunks, fresh or canned
   4 quarts orange sections
   1 quart whipped cream for dressing

SALADS WITH CANNED FRUITS

One of the less expensive and quickest methods of preparing fruit salads is to use canned fruits. When using fruit halves, the labels on the can should be read carefully for the count. A part of the juice from the canned fruits can be added to a cooked dressing or to an oil & fruit juice dressing, with the further addition of sour cream or whipped cream.

One No. 10 can should contain sufficient fruit for 25 salads, depending on the amount of liquid the fruit has.

The following suggestions for salad dressing can be used for canned or fresh fruit salads: (see Salad Dressings pp. 120ff)
1. A cooked dressing with part mayonnaise, 1 1/2 quarts for 50 servings.
2. A dressing made with fruit juice added to sour cream or whipped cream, 1 1/2 quarts for 50 servings.
3. French dressing with chili sauce, 1 1/2 quarts for 50 servings.

The following suggestions are given for portions, measurements, and combinations using canned fruits. The recipes can be altered or modified to suit the occasion. To make 1/2 cup for each of 50 servings, you will need from 8 to 10 quarts of salad.

1. Pear halves with cheese & orange marmalade
   2 No. 10 cans pear halves, well drained
   1 1/2 pounds shredded sharp cheese
   1 quart orange marmalade

2. Peach halves with Queen Ann cherries
   1 No. 10 can large peach halves, drained
   1 No. 10 can Queen Ann cherries, drained
   1 1/2 quarts dressing made with fruit juice and whipped cream

3. Apricots with grapefruit sections
   1 No. 10 can apricot halves, peeled and drained
   2 quarts grapefruit sections, drained
   1 quart pineapple chunks, drained
   1 1/2 quarts cooked dressing with mayonnaise

FROZEN FRUIT SALAD

To make approximately 50 medium-size slices

YOU WILL NEED
2 quarts mandarin orange sections, drained
2 quarts crushed pineapple
1 quart canned sliced peaches, drained
2 10-ounce packages frozen red raspberries, thawed
1 cup mayonnaise
3 cups heavy cream, whipped
2 cups fruit juices, a combination of those drained from the fruits

THE PREPARATION

Stir all of the ingredients together and fold in the whipped cream, stirring just enough to distribute the mixture. Taste for sweetness, and add about 1/2 cup sugar if needed. Turn into freezing pans or cartons and freeze overnight. Serve in individual servings on a bed of shredded lettuce. A mint leaf or a maraschino cherry makes a pretty garnish. No dressing is needed.

VARIATION I

Frozen fruit salad—25 servings
1 quart orange sections
4 cups sliced ripe bananas
1 quart sliced canned pears, drained
1 quart Bing cherries, pitted, drained
1/3 cup lemon juice
1/2 cup sugar
1 cup mayonnaise
3 cups heavy cream, whipped

Follow preparation directions as given above.

VARIATION II

Frozen fruit salad—for 50 servings
1 No. 10 can fruit cocktail, drained
1 10-ounce package frozen strawberries
4 cups tiny marshmallows
1 8-ounce package cream cheese, softened
1 cup mayonnaise
2 cups heavy cream, whipped
2 cups fruit juices, drained from fruit cocktail

To prepare, follow the directions as given above

VEGETABLE-FRUIT COMBINATIONS

Some suggested dressings for vegetable-fruit combinations:
(See salad dressings, pp. 120ff.)

1. 1 quart cooked dressing with 2 cups heavy cream, whipped
2. 1 1/2 quarts sesame seed dressing
3. 1 cup mayonnaise, 1 cup sweetened fruit juice, with 2 cups heavy cream, whipped
4. mayonnaise

WALDORF SALAD

To make approximately 50 servings

YOU WILL NEED
- 7 quarts Delicious apples, peeled, chilled, and diced
- 2 quarts thinly sliced celery hearts, chilled
- 3 cups English walnuts, chopped
- 1 quart cooked salad dressing, combined with 2 cups heavy cream, whipped
- 4 to 5 heads lettuce, shredded

THE PREPARATION

Prepare the celery ahead and refrigerate. Have the apples chilled and ready to peel and dice at the last minute, or prepare them in advance and sprinkle them with lemon juice to prevent discoloring. When ready to make the salad, combine all ingredients; toss them, do not stir. For a pretty garnish top each serving with a cooked, seeded and split prune stuffed with nuts.

VARIATION I

For apple combinations

- 6 quarts Delicious apples, peeled, and diced
- 4 cups raisins
- 2 quarts grated carrots
- Sugar as needed
- 1 1/2 quarts mayonnaise, fruit juice and whipped cream combined

VARIATION II

- 5 quarts Delicious apples, peeled and diced
- 2 quarts orange sections
- 2 quarts seedless grapes
- 1 1/2 quarts cooked salad dressing with 1 cup whipped cream

CARROT & RAISIN SALAD

To make approximately 50 servings

YOU WILL NEED
- 6 quarts grated fresh carrots
- 4 cups raisins
- 1 tablespoon salt
- 1/2 cup sugar
- 1/2 cup lemon juice
- 1 1/2 quarts mayonnaise

THE PREPARATION

Peel and grate the carrots, sprinkle with salt, add sugar, and refrigerate for about 1 hour. Combine with all other ingredients, toss lightly and serve either on a bed of shredded lettuce or in large chilled bowls. Garnish with orange slices.

VARIATION

Carrots, pineapple, and coconut
- 4 quarts grated fresh carrots
- 2 quarts crushed pineapple, drained
- 1 quart cooked salad dressing with 1 cup whipped cream
- 2 cups flaky coconut
- 1 teaspoon salt

VEGETABLE SALADS

TOSSED GREEN SALAD

When certain ingredients, such as tomatoes, hard-cooked eggs, croutons, or some other addition, are added to this tossed green it is usually labeled chef's salad. I suppose some chef got bored with the plain lettuce salad and found fame and fortune in making all types and kinds of additions to it. However, a crisp, fresh lettuce salad with an oil and vinegar dressing is still very popular and satisfying. A bulk salad of this sort usually requires generous helpings since it is not very filling.

To make approximately 50 servings

YOU WILL NEED
- 6 pounds head lettuce
- 2 pounds leaf lettuce, either romaine, Bibb, or garden variety
- 1 1/2 quarts French oil & vinegar dressing

THE PREPARATION

Have all of the lettuce thoroughly washed and chilled. Using a large wooden bowl, or small individual wooden bowls, break the lettuce into bite-size pieces. Sprinkle with the dressing and toss lightly.

VARIATION I

Reduce the amount of head lettuce by 1 pound and add 3 cups thinly shredded red cabbage. Toss with oil & vinegar dressing.

VARIATION II

Reduce the amount of head lettuce by 1 pound and add 2 cups finely grated carrots, and 1 cup shredded white cabbage. Toss with sesame seed dressing.

VARIATION III

Reduce the head lettuce by 2 pounds and add 1 cup sliced radishes and 1 quart ripe tomato wedges, and 1 cup thinly sliced onions. Toss with celery seed dressing.

And if the dish contentment brings,
You'll dine with me again.

A VEGETABLE SALAD

To make approximately 50 servings

YOU WILL NEED
- 4 quarts cooked and diced cauliflower
- 2 quarts English peas, cooked and drained
- 2 cups finely chopped celery
- 1/2 cup finely chopped onion
- 2 cups thinly sliced green pepper
- 1/2 cup finely chopped pimiento (can be used for garnish)
- 4 heads of lettuce shredded, for base
- 1 1/2 quarts sesame seed dressing

THE PREPARATION

Sprinkle the celery, onion, and green peppers with some of the dressing and set aside. Combine the cauliflower and English peas, which have been cooked and well drained, with the first mixture. Then toss lightly with the remainder of the dressing. Fold in the pimiento, or reserve it for the garnish. When ready to serve, lift the mixture with a slotted spoon onto a base of shredded lettuce. Serve immediately while the vegetables are still cold and crisp.

CABBAGE SALADS

COLE SLAW

To make approximately 50 servings of 1/2 cup each

YOU WILL NEED
- 8 quarts freshly shredded cabbage
- 1 1/2 cups sugar
- 1 3/4 cups white vinegar
- 3/4 cup water
- 3 tablespoons salt
- 4 tablespoons celery seed (optional)
- 1 cup finely sliced onion rings
- 2 teaspoons black pepper
- shredded red cabbage for garnish (optional)

THE PREPARATION

Shred the cabbage, sprinkle with salt, and add the water. Refrigerate for at least one hour. Combine all other ingredients, using celery seed and onion rings if desired, and pour the mixture over the cabbage, tossing it lightly. Refrigerate again until ready to serve, but toss from time to time to distribute the dressing flavor. Use a slotted spoon to remove from liquid when ready to serve. The red cabbage, finely shredded, sprinkled over the top makes a pretty garnish.

VARIATION I

Cabbage, carrots, and green peppers
6 quarts shredded cabbage
1 quart grated carrots
2 cups finely chopped green peppers
1/2 cup finely chopped onions
salt to taste, about 2 teaspoons
1 1/2 quarts French oil & vinegar dressing

VARIATION II

Cabbage-pineapple
6 quarts shredded cabbage
2 quarts chunk pineapple, diced and drained
1 1/2 quarts dressing, a combination of mayonnaise, pineapple juice, and whipped cream

VARIATION III

Cabbage with apples & raisins
6 quarts shredded cabbage
2 quarts Delicious apples, partially peeled and diced
2 cups raisins
2 teaspoons salt
1 1/2 quarts salad dressing, a combination of mayonnaise, orange juice, and whipped cream

POTATO SALAD

Of all church supper salads, surely potato salad takes first place, partly because it is the most filling and partly because it can serve more than one purpose. It not only supplements a meal, but can almost be the meal. Special caution should be taken in preparing this salad, however, because the fermentation element in potatoes combined with the oil in the dressing makes it inclined to spoil easily. I always chill the potatoes immediately after they are cooked and peeled, and before combining with the other ingredients.

To make 50 generous servings

YOU WILL NEED

14 to 15 pounds potatoes
3 tablespoons salt
3 tablespoons celery seed
12 hard-cooked eggs
1/3 cup grated fresh onion
1 cup chopped pimiento
1 1/2 cups finely chopped sweet pickles
1/3 cup vinegar
3 cups, or more, mayonnaise

THE PREPARATION

Cook the potatoes with the jackets on and, when they are completely tender, remove from heat and cool. When cool enough to handle, peel, slice or dice, and refrigerate for an hour or longer, or until chilled thoroughly. Combine with all other ingredients and chill again. Toss lightly when adding the dressing to keep the potatoes from becoming mushy. This salad should be made with the chunks defineable. Some of the pimiento and some of the hard-cooked eggs can be reserved and used as a garnish.

HOT POTATO SALAD
German-style

This recipe came to me straight from Germany years ago. I have made it dozens of times and shared it with many of my friends. I have also adapted it for quantity cooking, which all crowds seem to appreciate.

To make approximately 50 generous servings

YOU WILL NEED
- 14 pounds potatoes, cooked, peeled, and sliced
- 1 pound breakfast bacon, chopped
- 3 quarts hot beef, or chicken, stock
- 2 cups thinly sliced onions
- 1 cup vinegar
- 1/3 cup sugar
- 10 eggs hard-cooked
- salt, according to need
- 2 teaspoons black pepper

THE PREPARATION

Boil the potatoes with the jackets on, remove from hot water when they are quite tender. Cool, peel, and slice (do not dice). Have the stock boiling hot and set off the heat. Pour this over the sliced potatoes and let them marinate for at least 30 minutes. While the potatoes are marinating in the stock, chop the bacon and fry slowly in a large heavy kettle, turning often to prevent burning. When the bacon is crisp, remove it from the fat and add the onions to the fat and cook them until barely tender. Add the vinegar and sugar to the onion and fat mixture. Taste for salt before adding it, since the broth will have been salted. Add the pepper and with a slotted spoon lift the potatoes from the stock into the kettle with the fat mixture and return to the heat. Add the bacon and toss the mixture lightly as it is being reheated. Serve this salad *hot* on warm platters, surrounded by slices of hard-cooked eggs. Some of the eggs can be used for garnishing the top also.

SWEET POTATO SALAD

My niece, Gene Williams, of Laurel, Montana, gave me the recipe for this unusual salad and we have enjoyed it so much that I have adapted it for quantity cooking.

To make approximately 25 servings

YOU WILL NEED
- 2 pounds sweet potatoes after being cooked
- 1 1/2 cups minced celery
- 2 teaspoons salt
- 4 tablespoons grated onion
- 7 hard-cooked eggs, chopped
- 2 tablespoons French oil and vinegar dressing
- 1 cup mayonnaise
- 1/4 teaspoon white pepper

THE PREPARATION

Combine the sweet potatoes with the mayonnaise, French dressing, onion, salt, and pepper. Taste for seasonings. In the large bowl of an electric mixer, or by hand, beat the mixture until the potatoes are fluffy. Fold in the eggs and celery. Refrigerate for several hours. For an attractive garnish, fill green pepper rings with crumbled hard-cooked eggs, spread over top of the salad in design.

CHICKEN SALAD

To make approximately 50 servings

YOU WILL NEED
- 6 pounds cooked chicken, boned and cubed (about 18 pounds before cooking)
- 10 eggs, hard-cooked
- 3 cups seedless grapes or seeded grapes, sliced
- 1 quart finely chopped celery hearts
- salt and pepper
- 1 quart mayonnaise with 1/3 cup lemon juice

THE PREPARATION

If the chicken is salted while it is cooking, the salad may need only a sprinkle of salt after being put together. Taste to see. If time permits before combining the chicken with other ingredients, marinate it in some of the broth in which it was boiled. Lift the chicken pieces from the broth and combine with all other ingredients. Sprinkle with the pepper and salt, if needed. Toss lightly to keep the ingredients intact. Chill and serve on a base of crisp, shredded lettuce. The salad may need to be lifted out of the liquid with a slotted spoon when served.

VARIATION

5 to 6 pounds cooked, boned, and cubed chicken
2 cups almonds toasted and chopped
3 cups Queen Anne cherries, drained
1/3 cup lemon juice
2 cups thinly sliced celery hearts
2 1/2 cups cooked salad dressing with 2 cups whipped cream

SHRIMP SALAD

To make approximately 50 servings

YOU WILL NEED
8 pounds cooked, deveined shrimp, chopped
1/2 cup lemon juice
1 tablespoon prepared mustard
4 cups finely diced celery
2 tablespoons grated onion (optional)
1 cup finely diced sweet pickle
3 cups mayonnaise
2 teaspoons salt
1 teaspoon black pepper

THE PREPARATION

Prepare the shrimp and refrigerate while preparing the other ingredients. Combine all ingredients and toss until well-blended. Chill before serving. Serve on a bed of shredded lettuce.

VARIATION

6 pounds cooked, deveined shrimp, chilled
2 pounds potatoes, cooked, diced, chilled
4 teaspoons salt
1 teaspoon white pepper
2 cups finely diced celery
1/3 cup lemon juice
1 quart mayonnaise

TUNA SALAD

Salmon or bonita can be substituted in this recipe for the tuna, using equal amounts as given.

To make approximately 50 servings

YOU WILL NEED

8 pounds flaked tuna, well drained and rinsed if it has an oil base
10 hard-cooked eggs
1 1/2 quarts mayonnaise
1/3 cup lemon juice
3 cups thinly sliced celery hearts
2 cups finely chopped sweet pickles

THE PREPARATION

Combine all ingredients and toss lightly to distribute them well without mashing the tuna. Chill well before serving. Serve on a bed of shredded lettuce, and use slices of pimiento and hard-cooked eggs for the garnish.

VARIATION

8 pounds flaked tuna or salmon
8 hard-cooked eggs
4 cups diced ripe apples
1/2 cup lemon juice
1 tablespoon prepared mustard
1/3 cup finely chopped onion
1 quart mayonnaise

CONGEALED SALADS

When making congealed salads for large crowds, mold them in oblong pans and cut into squares for individual servings. Of course, the individual mold is always in order, especially if a special shape or size is desired. The amount of gelatin needed to make a good mold varies; the more acid content that is in the ingredients the more gelatin is required. If the gelatin is needed quickly, reduce the amount of water and/or increase the amount of the gelatin. It requires more gelatin to congeal a salad in hot weather than in cold.

The yield of congealed salad. One gallon of gelatin base (the water and the gelatin) with approximately 3 quarts of solid ingredients, fruits, vegetables or a combination (fresh pineapple WILL NOT congeal) will yield about 55 servings of 2 1/2-inch squares. One oblong pan 16 x 10 inches cuts about 28 servings of this size.

To make one gallon base with flavored gelatin. To one gallon boiling water stir in 26 ounces 8 or 9 3-ounce packages of flavored gelatin of any good brand. Add the ingredients as directed above.

To make one gallon base of unflavored granulated gelatin. To one gallon boiling water stir in 7 1/2 to 10 tablespoons of unflavored gelatin after it has been dissolved in 2 or 3 cups cold water. Unflavored gelatin comes in packages containing 1 tablespoon each. Add ingredients as directed above.

CHICKEN CONSOMME MOLD

This is a good salad to make in very small molds and serve as an appetizer, or as a first course instead of a soup.

To make 50 servings, of approximately 4-ounces each

YOU WILL NEED
- 7 1-tablespoon packages of unflavored gelatin
- 1 quart cold water
- 3 quarts chicken consommé
- 1 cup finely chopped sweet pickles
- 1 cup mayonnaise
- 10 hard-cooked eggs, finely chopped
- 1 cup thinly sliced celery hearts
- 1 cup thinly sliced stuffed olives
- 1 cup thinly sliced pimiento for garnish
- lettuce leaf for base, about 4 heads

THE PREPARATION

Sprinkle the gelatin over the cold water and set aside until dissolved. Bring the 3 quarts of consommé to a boil and, when the gelatin has dissolved, add to the hot consommé. Stir until the mixture is smooth and blended. Add all other ingredients, except the pimiento. Mold in small individual molds which have been rinsed in cold water. Refrigerate several hours before serving. Unmold on a lettuce leaf, and garnish with a strip of pimiento.

PEAR AND CHEESE MOLD

To make approximately 50 servings

YOU WILL NEED
- 50 pear halves, or about 4 1/2 pounds sliced pears, drained
- 2 quarts boiling water
- 24 ounces, or 8 3-ounce packages lime flavored gelatin
- 2 quarts pear juice, or a combination of pear juice and water
- 1/3 cup lemon juice
- 1 pound cottage cheese, sieved and creamed
- lettuce for base

THE PREPARATION

Dissolve the gelatin in the boiling water and stir until blended. Add fruit juice. Have the mold or molds ready for use, and if using the pear halves instead of sliced pears, place them carefully on the bottom of whatever molds are being used. Refrigerate the gelatin mixture while preparing the cheese. Sieve the cheese, or put through a blender. It should be smooth and creamy. Add lemon juice to the cheese, and when the gelatin begins to thicken, stir in the cheese. Keep stirring until smooth. Pour the thickened gelatin over the pear halves and refrigerate for several hours before serving. (If sliced pears are used, they can be added any time.) Poppy seed dressing, or a combination of cooked dressing with poppy seed, makes an excellent finish to this delicious salad. Serve on a bed of shredded lettuce.

VARIATION

24 ounces, or 8 3-ounce packages orange gelatin
2 quarts boiling water
2 quarts fruit juice, drained from fruits being used
1 quart mandarin orange sections, drained
1 quart grapefruit sections
2 cups seedless white grapes

Follow preparation directions as given above.

'Tis an old maxim in the schools,
That flattery's the food of fools;
Yet now and then your men of wit
will condescend to take a bit.
—Swift

SALAD DRESSINGS

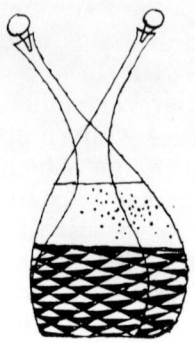

The guide lines for which dressing to use for what salad are as varied as the salads for which they are made. Each cook will have to be her own judge as to which one to use for a particular salad. I am giving here a few suggestions which may help in determining such decisions.

A tart French dressing goes well with tossed green vegetable salads, or can be used for marinating vegetables. Tart and sweet French dressings go well with fruits or combination of fruits and vegetales.

Mayonnaise and salad dressing combinations compliment seafood salads, egg salads, and most molded salads.

A cooked salad dressing goes especially well with a potato salad, and with some combinations of fruits. A sweet-and-sour cooked dressing enhances fruits and melon combinations.

A sour cream dressing adds much to a fruit or fruit and vegetable combination.

Cheese added to dressings is used most often to give substance to lettuce wedges or to other greens.

FRENCH DRESSING
a basic recipe

Many people call every dressing French whether it deserves the title or not. If the base of the dressing is oil and vinegar, or oil and lemon juice, and seasonings (no matter what the seasonings), it can rightfully be called French.

To make approximately 1 1/2 quarts

YOU WILL NEED
1 pint white vinegar
1 quart salad oil
1 tablespoon salt
1 teaspoon white pepper
2 tablespoons sugar
1 tablespoon prepared mustard
1 teaspoon paprika

THE PREPARATION

Mix or shake all ingredients together vigorously until well-blended. Or put the ingredients through a blender. When time permits, make the dressing ahead and let it age a bit. It improves as it ages.

VARIATION I

French dressing with fruit juices, 1 1/2 quarts
1 cup white vinegar
1/2 cup orange juice
1/2 cup juice from canned peaches or apricots
1 quart salad oil
2 teaspoons salt
2 teaspoons prepared mustard
1 tablespoon grated onion
2 tablespoons sugar

Beat until well-blended.

VARIATION II

French dressing with poppy seed, sesame seed, or celery seed approximately 2 quarts
3 cups sugar
2 cups white vinegar
1 1/2 quarts salad oil
3 tablespoons grated onion
2 tablespoons prepared mustard
3 tablespoons poppy seed, or 2 tablespoons celery seed, or 2 tablespoons toasted sesame seed
1/2 teaspoon salt

Beat until well-blended

VARIATION III

French dressing with chili sauce, 1 1/2 quarts
1 cup chili sauce, bottled
1/2 cup sugar
1 cup white vinegar
3 cups salad oil
1 teaspoon salt
2 tablespoons grated onion
1/2 teaspoon paprika
1/4 teaspoon cayenne pepper (optional)

Beat until well-blended

MAYONNAISE DRESSING
a basic recipe

This is a smooth, creamy dressing, made by beating the oil very slowly into the seasoned vinegar and egg mixture. It is added slowly to prevent separating. Bold or mild seasonings may be used, depending on taste. It can be made days ahead and refrigerated, and if it should separate, it can be beaten again, and one or more egg yolks added to bring it back to its proper consistency.

To make approximately 1 1/2 quarts

YOU WILL NEED
- 4 egg yolks
- 1 tablespoon salt
- 1 teaspoon paprika
- 1 tablespoon prepared mustard
- 1/2 cup vinegar
- 1 1/2 quarts salad oil

THE PREPARATION

Place the egg yolks, salt, paprika, and mustard in a large mixing bowl. Beat until the mixture is well blended and slightly thick. Add the vinegar and stir until smooth. Start adding the oil, little by little, beating well after each addition. Continue the process until all of the oil has been added. The mixture should form a thick emulsion.

VARIATION I

Blue Cheese Mayonnaise—approximately 1 quart
- 2 cups mayonnaise dressing, as given above
- 1 cup blue cheese, crumbled
- 1/2 cup milk
- 1/4 cup lemon juice
- sprinkle of Tabasco sauce

Mix all ingredients together and beat until blended

VARIATION II

Mayonnaise with cucumbers—approximately 1 1/2 quarts
- 1 quart mayonnaise dressing, as given above
- 1 cup grated cucumbers, seeds removed, and drained
- 1 cup heavy cream, whipped
- 1/2 teaspoon salt
- 1/3 cup lemon juice

Mix all ingredients together and beat until blended

VARIATION III

Thousand Island dressing—approximately 1 1/2 quarts

1 quart mayonnaise dressing, as given on p. 123
1 cup bottled chili sauce
6 hard-cooked eggs, chopped
1 cup finely chopped celery
2 tablespoons grated onion
1/2 cup finely chopped dill pickle
2 tablespoons minced pimiento

Mix all ingredients together and beat until blended

COOKED SALAD DRESSING

A cooked salad dressing has a white sauce base and in addition, eggs, vinegar (or lemon juice), oil or butter, and a variety of seasonings. It should be creamy and have a tart, zippy flavor. It can be seasoned according to taste and in keeping with the salad being served.

To make approximately 2 quarts

YOU WILL NEED

1 quart milk
2 cups water
1/4 cup butter or margarine
1 cup vinegar
1/2 cup sugar
1/2 cup flour
2 teaspoons salt
2 tablespoons prepared mustard
1/4 teaspoon cayenne pepper (optional)
6 eggs, well-beaten

THE PREPARATION

Mix all dry ingredients together. Blend them well. Add the water and stir until you have a smooth pastelike mixture. Add the beaten eggs to the mixture and blend. Bring the milk to a boil, but do not boil, then gradually combine the mixtures. Cook the mixture over low heat for about 15 minutes, stirring constantly. Add the mustard, vinegar, and butter and beat until thoroughly blended. This makes an excellent dressing for cabbage or for a cabbage and fruit combination, as well as for many other salads.

VARIATION I

Fruit salad dressing, approximately 1 1/2 quarts
1 quart cooked dressing, see basic recipe
1 cup orange juice
1 cup pineapple juice
1/3 cup lemon juice
2 cups heavy cream, whipped and slightly sweetened

Mix all ingredients together and blend well.

VARIATION II

Sour cream with cooked dressing, approximately 2 quarts
1 quart cooked dressing, see basic recipe
1 quart cultured sour cream
1/2 cup honey

Mix all ingredients together and blend well.

SAUCES FOR MEATS AND VEGETABLES

WHITE SAUCE
a basic recipe

For a thin white sauce. To 2 quarts milk, use 1/2 cup butter, 1/2 cup flour, 2 teaspoons salt.
For a medium sauce. To 2 quarts milk, use 3/4 cup butter, 3/4 cup flour, 2 teaspoons salt.
For a thick sauce. To 2 quarts milk, use 1 1/4 cups butter, 1 1/2 cups flour, 2 teaspoons salt.

THE PREPARATION

Melt the butter over low heat, remove from fire, and stir in the flour, stirring until perfectly smooth. Add the salt. Scald the milk and gradually add to flour mixture. Return to heat and cook slowly for about 15 minutes, stirring constantly until the milk is smooth and reaches the required thickness.

VARIATION I

Mushroom sauce, approximately 2 1/2 quarts
2 quarts medium white sauce
2 cups sliced mushrooms, sautéed in butter
1 tablespoon grated onion
2 tablespoons minced green peppers
2 tablespoons minced pimiento

Combine and blend

VARIATION II

Egg sauce, approximately 2 quarts
2 quarts medium white sauce
10 hard-cooked eggs, chopped
1 tablespoon prepared mustard
2 tablespoons hot horseradish

Combine and blend. Serve over salmon loaf, baked tuna, fish, or vegetables.

VARIATION III

Cheese sauce, approximately 2 quarts
2 quarts thick white sauce
1 pound sharp Cheddar cheese, grated
2 tablespoons Worcestershire sauce
a sprinkle of Tabasco sauce

Combine and blend. Serve over soufflés, fish dishes, or vegetables.

BROWN SAUCE

To make approximately 2 1/2 quarts

YOU WILL NEED
2 quarts meat stock, chicken or beef
1 cup fat meat drippings, beef, pork, or chicken
1 cup flour, browned
salt, if necessary
1/2 teaspoon black pepper
1/2 cup finely chopped onion (optional)

THE PREPARATION

Do not salt the sauce until made, then taste to see if needed. The fat and the stock will have been salted. In a heavy large kettle or skillet, brown the flour by cooking over low heat, and stirring constantly until the flour is browned sufficiently. Pour the flour into a bowl and set aside. In the same skillet, or kettle, melt the fat (or drippings) and gradually stir in the flour. Add pepper and onions, if desired. Gradually stir in the meat stock and cook slowly for about 15 minutes, stirring occasionally, until the mixture is smooth and thick.

VARIATION

A sweet brown sauce, approximately 2 quarts
2 quarts brown sauce
1 cup currant jelly, melted
1 tablespoon white vinegar
1 teaspoon fresh grated onion

Combine and blend. Serve with lamb, wild game, pork ribs, or ham.

BÉCHAMEL SAUCE

This is one of the basic French sauces with many uses. It is a standard in French cuisine.

To make approximately 2 1/2 quarts

YOU WILL NEED
1 quart milk, hot
3/4 cup butter
1/2 cup flour
6 cups chicken stock
1/3 cup finely diced onion
1/2 cup chopped carrots
1 bay leaf
1/2 teaspoon thyme
1 tablespoon peppercorns
1 teaspoon white pepper
salt, if necessary

THE PREPARATION

Combine all ingredients except the hot milk, butter, and flour. Cook them slowly for about 30 minutes. Melt the butter, and stir in the flour until well blended and smooth. Gradually add the hot milk and stir until smooth. Strain the cooked stock mixture and combine the mixtures. Cook again, slowly, stirring occasionally, until smooth and thick. Excellent served over soufflés, fish dishes, and chicken.

MORNAY SAUCE

This is a good sauce to serve over a thin slice of hot turkey or chicken breast with a slice of hot toast under all. Its base is Béchamel sauce, which accounts for the delicious flavor.

To make approximately 2 quarts

YOU WILL NEED
- 1 1/2 quarts hot Béchamel sauce
- 1 tablespoon Worcestershire sauce
- a pinch of cayenne pepper
- 1 cup grated sharp cheese
- 1 cup grated Parmesan cheese
- 1/2 cup butter

THE PREPARATION

Over hot water heat the Béchamel sauce and add all other ingredients, cooking slowly until the cheeses are completely blended with the other ingredients. Serve while hot. A sprinkle of paprika over each serving adds an attractive touch.

PARSLEY-BUTTER SAUCE
a basic recipe

To make about 2 cups, melt 1 pound of butter and stir in 1/2 cup finely chopped fresh parsley. Serve over new potatoes, certain vegetables and fish.

VARIATION I

Lemon-almond butter sauce
- 1 cup melted butter
- 2 tablespoons finely chopped parsley
- 1/3 cup lemon juice
- 1/2 teaspoon grated lemon rind
- 1/2 cup finely chopped toasted almonds

Combine and serve over asparagus, artichokes, fish, etc.

VARIATION II

Mint-butter sauce
1 cup melted butter
1 tablespoon finely chopped fresh mint leaves
1/3 cup lemon juice

Combine and serve hot over lamb

VARIATION III

Vegetable stock sauce
1 cup melted butter
2 cups vegetable stock, well-seasoned
1/4 cup lemon juice
1/2 teaspoon dried herbs

Combine and serve hot over vegetables.

HOT MUSTARD SAUCE

This is a tart, rich sauce and is good to serve with cold slices of pork or beef roast. It can be used sparingly on sandwiches as a spread with sliced chicken breasts or beef cuts.

To make approximately 1 1/2 pints

YOU WILL NEED
1 pint heavy cream, whipped
1/3 cup lemon juice
2 tablespoons water
4 tablespoons prepared hot mustard
sprinkle of salt
2 tablespoons sugar
2 eggs, beaten
2 tablespoons margarine or butter

THE PREPARATION

Beat the eggs, lemon juice, and water together until blended. Add all other ingredients except the cream and butter. Cook the mixture over hot water until thick, stirring constantly. Set off the heat, add the butter, and chill. When the mixture is thoroughly chilled, fold in the whipped cream. This sauce can be stored in the refrigerator for several days without loss of substance or flavor.

TOMATO SAUCE

By adding some Italian spices, such as thyme, oregano, bay leaf, and others, this sauce can be served over meat balls, spaghetti, and many other meat dishes, as well as certain vegetables.

To make approximately 2 1/2 quarts

YOU WILL NEED
- 2 quarts canned tomatoes, chopped
- 1/2 cup butter
- 1/2 cup flour
- 2 tablespoons grated fresh onion
- 3 tablespoons sugar
- 1 teaspoon salt
- 2 teaspoons Worcestershire sauce
- 1/8 teaspoon Tabasco sauce

THE PREPARATION

Add the seasonings to the tomatoes and cook slowly for about 20 minutes. Melt the butter and gradually stir in the flour. Cook slowly until blended, about 5 minutes. Stir in the tomato mixture gradually and cook until thickened, about 10 minutes.

VARIATION

Chili-tomato sauce, approximately 2 quarts
- 2 quarts tomato sauce, as given above
- 4 tablespoons chili powder
- 1/2 teaspoon cumin powder
- 1/3 cup finely chopped green chili peppers

Combine and serve hot with red beans, and ground meats.

COCKTAIL SAUCE

The perfect sauce to serve over shrimp, crab, oysters, other fish dishes, and certain vegetables and vegetable salads.

To make approximately 2 quarts

YOU WILL NEED
- 1 quart bottled chili sauce
- 1 cup lemon juice
- 2 cups tomato catsup
- 1 tablespoon grated onion
- 2 tablespoons Worcestershire sauce
- 2 tablespoons hot horseradish
- 2 tablespoons sugar, or more
- sprinkle of Tabasco sauce

THE PREPARATION

Blend all ingredients together and chill. This sauce can be stored in refrigerator indefinitely.

BARBECUE SAUCE

Every cookbook must have a barbecue sauce recipe, or so it seems. This sauce does serve many purposes and can be especially helpful and practical in quantity cooking.

To make approximately 2 quarts

YOU WILL NEED
- 6 cups tomato catsup
- 1 cup water
- 1/3 cup lemon juice
- 1 teaspoon salt
- 2 tablespoons brown sugar
- 1 tablespoon grated fresh onion
- 1/4 cup melted margarine
- 1 tablespoon Worcestershire sauce
- 1/4 teaspoon Tabasco sauce

THE PREPARATION

Combine all ingredients and cook over low heat for about 15 minutes, stirring occasionally. Use to baste as the meat is roasting, baking, or cooking.

> He may live without books,—what is knowledge but grieving?
> He may live without hope,—what is hope but deceiving?
> He may live without love,—what is passion but pining?
> But where is the man that can live without dining?
> —Owen Meredith

SANDWICHES

Good, appetizing sandwiches can fill many needs, not only for a church supper but for other quantity meals as well. They can provide the base of the main meal, or supplement it. The bread, if it is homemade (churchmade), will add a great deal of zest to the sandwich. The bread used for the sandwiches should provide not only nourishment, but color, flavor, texture, and a satisfying taste.

Preparing sandwiches ahead. Sandwiches can be frozen, with but a few exceptions, or they can be stored easily in the refrigerator for a few hours. When freezing sandwiches or when storing them, they should be wrapped in separate sandwich paper bags. If the bags are not available, the sandwiches can be wrapped in waxed paper or foil, and a damp cloth placed over the outside of the paper or foil.

To make the sandwiches. First determine the bread and then the spread and filling. There is whole wheat, white, pumpernickel, French, and Boston brown bread to choose from. And there is raisin bread, a sweet loaf, hamburger bun and many sweet breads which are appropriate for sweet sandwiches. Next is the spread, such as a thin spread of softened butter or margarine, mayonnaise or salad dressing, or perhaps a cooked salad dressing. Of course, there is always mustard and horseradish.

Fillings. The Danish people boast of hundreds of fillings and spreads for their open sandwich. They spread and serve just about anything and everything on a large single slice of bread, cut lengthwise of the loaf, and usually garnished with crisp, fresh vegetables. We can duplicate their production of a sandwich if we give extra care in selecting a good bread. See Danish Open Sandwiches, p. 232.

Fillings for 50 sandwiches. Prepare approximately 2 quarts of a filling for 50 sandwiches, allowing 1 1/2 to 2 tablespoons for each sandwich for average bread slice.

The following suggested fillings are for almost any style, shape, or size sandwich:
1. Egg, hard-cooked, chopped, with stuffed chopped olives and a spread of mayonnaise.
2. Ground, cold boiled tongue, highly seasoned and with a mayonnaise spread.
3. Minced dried beef, mixed with mayonnaise, seasoned with horseradish, and spread on rye bread.
4. Cream cheese with grated cubumbers, combined with cooked, highly seasoned salad dressing.
5. Cottage cheese, well-drained and beaten until smooth, seasoned with grated onion, ground green peppers, and served on rye or whole wheat breads.
6. For a sweet sandwich, use finely chopped nuts, cream cheese and chopped dates, thinned with a little lemon juice. Serve on raisin bread.

The following are suggested fillings for toasted or grilled sandwiches:
1. Meat, fish, or poultry with a salad dressing to bind the mixture.
2. A slice of tomato with crisp bacon, and a spread of mayonnaise.

3. Swiss cheese on rye bread with a mayonnaise spread.
4. Sliced corned beef, tomato, and lettuce on rye or whole wheat bread.
5. Sliced ham, with thinly sliced dill pickle and spread with mustard.
6. Chicken livers, cooked with seasonings, mashed and mixed with minced sweet pickles, and a salad dressing spread.

GRILLED CHEESE SANDWICHES

To make 50 sandwiches

YOU WILL NEED
3 1/2 pounds cheese, thinly sliced
1 pound melted butter, or 1 quart mayonnaise
100 slices white or whole wheat bread

THE PREPARATION

Spread the slices of bread with either melted butter or the mayonnaise. Place the slice of cheese between two slices of the bread and grill, or toast in hot oven.

VARIATION

Pimiento cheese for 50 sandwiches
1 1/2 cups finely chopped pimiento
3 1/2 pounds sharp or Swiss cheese, ground or grated
2 cups cooked salad dressing, or mayonnaise
1/4 teaspoon Tabasco sauce
100 slices bread, white or whole wheat

Grill, serve plain, or heat in hot oven for 20 minutes, at 450°. Serve immediately.

HAMBURGERS

To make 50 hamburgers, average size

50 hamburger buns
12 to 15 pounds ground beef, without fat

3 tablespoons salt
2 teaspoons black pepper
1 quart thinly sliced onions (optional)
1 1/2 quarts mayonnaise, or a combination of mustard and mayonnaise

Amounts of trimmings for 50 hamburgers

12 to 14 ripe tomatoes
2 dozen large dill pickles
4 to 5 heads crisp lettuce

OTHER POPULAR SANDWICHES

Amounts for ham salad sandwiches for 50

4 pounds ham, cooked and ground
1 cup finely chopped celery
1 cup sweet pickles, finely diced
6 eggs, hard-cooked, chopped
100 slices bread, white, rye or whole wheat
1 1/2 quarts mayonnaise
lettuce—optional

Amounts for a sweet ham sandwich for 50

4 pounds baked ham, finely chopped or ground
1/2 cup raisins, ground
1/2 cup crushed pineapple, drained
2 tablespoons lemon juice
1 cup finely chopped stuffed olives
100 slices bread, white or whole wheat
1 quart mayonnaise

Amounts for 50 tuna salad sandwiches

4 pounds tuna, flaked
8 hard-cooked eggs, chopped
3 tablespoons grated onion
1/3 cup lemon juice
1 1/2 cups cooked salad dressing
salt to taste—if needed
100 slices bread, white or whole wheat
lettuce—optional

Amounts for 50 chicken salad sandwiches

4 pounds chicken, cooked, boned, and cubed
salt, if needed
1/3 cup lemon juice
1 cup minced celery
1 1/2 cups mayonnaise
100 slices bread, white or whole wheat
lettuce—optional

or

4 pounds chicken, cooked, boned, and ground
10 eggs, hard-cooked, chopped
1 cup minced sweet pickle
1/2 cup minced pimiento
1 1/2 cups cooked salad dressing
100 slices bread, white or whole wheat
lettuce—optional
salt, if needed

REUBEN SANDWICH

This is considered one of the favorite heavy sandwiches. It is appetizing and filling and is often served as the main dish on the menu. It can also be the meal. Rye bread is the rule for making this sandwich, unless some other dark bread is preferred.

To make 50 hot Reuben sandwiches

YOU WILL NEED

50 slices rye bread, cut length-wise of the loaf
3 cups sandwich spread, either mustard or a seasoned mayonnaise
1 pound melted butter for basic spread (optional)
5 pounds corned beef, cooked and thinly sliced
2 quarts sauerkraut, drained
3 1/2 pounds Swiss cheese, thinly sliced
15 or 16 large dill pickles, strips for garnish

THE PREPARATION

Place the sauerkraut in a large sieve and set aside to drain. Slice the rye bread and spread first with melted butter and then with the mustard or mayonnaise dressing. Place the meat on the slice next, then 2 tablespoons, or more, of the sauerkraut, and then the cheese on the sauerkraut. Place the sandwiches on cookie sheets, or baking pans, and slide into a very hot oven, 450°, long enough to heat through and melt the cheese. Serve immediately. The dill pickle makes a nice garnish, and a small wedge of lettuce may be added also.

MEATS

BEEF

Roasting beef is referred to when meat is cooked in the oven without a cover, and without adding liquid. However, *roasting* and *baking* are used interchangeably, and the cook should not be too concerned if she uses both terms referring to the same piece of beef being prepared.

Beef roast. Cooked in the oven, uncovered and without liquid, at 300° for about 18 to 20 minutes per pound for rare meat; 22 to 25 minutes per pound for medium; and 27 to 30 minutes per pound for well done.

Baked beef. Cook in the oven with some liquid, covered and cooked at the same temperature, with the same time per pound as for *roast beef.*

Broiling beef. This method is usually for rib; club; T-bones; porterhouse; tenderloin, or sirloin steaks, which require different timing per pound for rare, medium, and well done, depending, of course, on thickness, size, and age of the beef. An average would be 1-inch thickness, cooked at 15 minutes per pound for rare; 20 minutes per pound for medium; and 30 minutes per pound for well done.

Panbroiling. This is my way of cooking steaks for crowds. I leave the real broiling to the experts in the big restaurants. Panbroiling is more predictable for me and in the long run less expensive. It is done by preheating an ungreased griddle or heavy frying pan, first browning quickly, and then reducing the heat to cook slowly. The steaks should be turned as needed to cook evenly on both sides. Make tests for desired doneness.

Braising. This method is especially good for the tougher cuts of meats. Dredge the meats first in flour, salt, and pepper. Use about 1/2 teaspoon salt per pound of meat. Cook the meat in a kettle or in a roasting pan with hot fat to brown on both sides and then add 4 or 5 cups of water, meat stock, or vegetable stock. Cook the meat about 45 minutes per pound, depending on the thickness and age of the beef. For a 5-pound roast, cook about 3 or 4 hours, covered. *For braising Swiss steaks,* about 2 inches thick, follow this same method and cook about 2 hours or a little longer.

Stewing and simmering. This method means keeping the heat below the boiling point. The meat is cooked in liquid for an average of 40 to 50 minutes per pound, depending on thickness and age of the meat. Cook in a heavy kettle with a tight-fitting lid.

BRISKET IN WINE

Of all the roasts, baked beef, or other cuts of beef that I prepare for my family, friends, or groups, this recipe is the most popular. It is slightly expensive and it may not always be practical for church suppers but, when the budget and time permits, do try it.

To make approximately 25 servings

YOU WILL NEED
10 to 12 pounds brisket, trimmed
4 cups Burgundy wine
2 to 3 tablespoons salt
sprinkle of black pepper
6 tablespoons Worcestershire sauce
1 pound breakfast bacon, sliced

THE PREPARATION

Line a large, heavy roaster with heavy foil (not extra heavy). Extend the foil on both sides and at the ends sufficient to cover the roast and secure it after it is ready to wrap. Lay the brisket or briskets on the foil and pour the wine over slowly. Salt and pepper. (The wine has a tendency to give a salty flavor, therefore, salt with caution.) Sprinkle the Worcestershire sauce over the meat, then lay slices of bacon over the top, covering the entire brisket with the strips of bacon. Fold the foil over the roast carefully and secure it by pressing the edges together. This roast does best when placed in the refrigerator for several hours or overnight, before baking. The wine tenderizes the meat and adds a delightful flavor when marinated ahead of cooking. When ready to cook, place in a preheated oven at 425° and bake at that temperature for just long enough to heat the meat thoroughly, about 30 minutes. Reduce the heat to 300° and cook for 4 to 5 hours, testing after about 3 hours. Some cuts become quite tender at 3 hours. The finished brisket should be very moist, tender enough to cut with a fork, with a full, delightful flavor.

CHOPPED SIRLOIN STEAKS

To make 50 servings of 4 to 5 ounces each

YOU WILL NEED
15 to 16 pounds coarsely ground sirloin, all lean
3 tablespoons salt
2 teaspoons black pepper
1 to 1 1/2 pounds margarine or other fat

THE PREPARATION

Mix the seasonings well into the meat, pat into oval cakes about 1/2 to 3/4 inches thick, and divide into required number of servings. In a heavy skillet, or skillets, heat a small amount of fat until hot but not smoking. Cook the steaks quickly until barely brown, turning once or twice to cook evenly. If the steaks must be kept for a time before serving, place them in a large roaster with fitting lid and keep in an oven with a temperature of about 250°. Serve them with a bit of their own liquid spooned over each. A hot mustard sauce goes well with these steaks.

VARIATION

Green-pepper steaks. Follow the recipe given above and, as the steaks come from the skillet, place them in a shallow baking pan. Have prepared ahead about 1 quart of minced green peppers, blended with 1/2 teaspoon Tabasco sauce. Place 1 tablespoon of this green mixture on top of each steak, slide under the broiler just long enough to cook the peppers and saturate the steaks with the flavor, about 5 or 10 minutes.

BEEF STROGANOFF WITH NOODLES

To make approximately 50 servings

YOU WILL NEED

10 to 12 pounds beef, top round or round steaks, cut into thin strips
2 pounds tiny noodles, cooked in meat broth
1 1/2 cups margarine
1 1/2 cups flour
1 cup finely chopped onions
2 1/2 quarts beef or chicken stock
1 pound mushrooms, sliced
2 tablespoons salt
2 quarts sour cream
3 tablespoons caraway seed
1/2 teaspoon nutmeg

THE PREPARATION

Melt the fat and brown the beef strips, turning them and shaking the skillet to brown evenly. Cook until just tender. While they brown, sprinkle them with the salt and some black pepper. Add the onions just before the strips are done, and allow them to cook until transparent. Add the flour and stir until thoroughly blended. Heat the broth and combine the two mixtures. Cook over low heat for about 20 minutes, or until the mixture blends. Fold in the seasonings, mushrooms, and sour cream. Taste for seasoning, add more salt if needed. Let the total mixture become hot, but do not boil. Serve over tiny noodles which have been cooked in a meat broth and seasoned with salt and white pepper to taste. Garnish with a sprig of parsley.

MEAT BALLS AND SPAGHETTI

To make approximately 50 servings

YOU WILL NEED

8 to 9 pounds ground beef, round preferred
3 to 4 pounds ground pork
2 tablespoons salt
1 teaspoon black pepper
3 cups bread crumbs
2 cups milk
3 to 4 pounds spaghetti, cooked in meat broth and seasoned

The sauce:
4 quarts canned tomatoes, peeled and chopped
1/2 teaspoon cayenne pepper
2 teaspoons salt
3 quarts boiling water
3 tablespoons sugar
1 cup finely chopped onions
1/2 cup bacon fat or margarine
2 tablespoons paprika
1/3 cup Worcestershire sauce
2 garlic cloves (optional)

THE PREPARATION

Make the sauce first by combining all of the ingredients and simmering for about 1 hour, or until the sauce is completely blended and slightly thick. Taste for seasonings and adjust as needed. Prepare the meat balls by blending the two meats together. Add salt and pepper. Soak crumbs in milk and add to meat mixture. Combine the ingredients quickly, because too much handling of ground meats tends to create a denseness in them. With the hands form the meat into balls, about 1 1/2 inches in diameter, making about 150, or 3 for each serving. Place them in baking pans and brown in a hot 450° oven, quickly, shake the pans as they cook to brown evenly. Remove the balls to a deep roaster with fitting lid. Pour the sauce over them, cover and cook for about 30 minutes at 350°. Serve over the cooked, hot spaghetti which has been seasoned and cooked in a meat broth.

VARIATION

To make Spanish meat balls add 4 tablespoons of chili powder and 1 teaspoon cumin powder to the sauce.

MEAT LOAF

To make approximately 50 servings or 5 medium loaves

YOU WILL NEED
- 8 to 9 pounds ground beef, round preferred
- 2 pounds ground fresh pork
- 4 cups bread crumbs
- 10 eggs, separated
- 3 tablespoons salt
- 1/4 teaspoon cayenne pepper
- 2 tablespoons grated fresh onion
- 1/4 cup Worcestershire sauce
- 2 quarts milk
- tomato catsup for top

THE PREPARATION

Blend the meats together and sprinkle with the salt and cayenne pepper. Add all other ingredients to the meat except the egg whites and tomato catsup. Beat the egg whites until stiff and fold them into the meat mixture; fold carefully but do not stir. The loaf will be light and the texture loose if the egg whites can be added without breaking them down. Pour the mixture into 5 well-greased loaf pans, average size, spread the catsup over each and bake in a preheated oven at 325° for about 1 to 1 1/2 hours, or until the loaf springs back when touched in the center and is slightly brown.

VARIATION

A very special variation is to divide 1 quart of sour cream into five parts. Spread each part over a loaf of the meat, and slice 3 cups of stuffed olives and spread over the cream. The olives can be placed in a design. The cream is added just before baking instead of the tomato catsup.

BEEF POT ROAST

To make 50 servings of 3 to 4 ounces each

YOU WILL NEED
- 18 to 20 pounds, boneless beef, top round or rump roast
- 3 tablespoons salt
- 2 teaspoons black pepper
- 2 quarts water

Gravy:
- 1 cup flour
- 1 1/2 cups cold water

THE PREPARATION

Sprinkle salt and pepper over the roast, rubbing it in well. Place in a large roaster in a very hot oven, about 450°, until the roast has browned. Turn to brown on all sides. Add about 2 quarts of water, cover with a tight-fitting lid and reduce the heat to 325°. Cook for 4 to 5 hours, checking occasionally to see if liquid is needed. Test for doneness before removing from oven. Make a gravy by mixing the flour in the cold water and stir until smooth and pastelike. Add this to the hot roast liquid and stir until smooth and well blended. Cook for about 5 minutes. The roast should cool about 30 minutes before it is sliced. It will fall apart if sliced when it is too hot.

VARIATION

Suitable vegetables may be added to the roast near the end of the baking, added in time for the particular vegetable to cook. Vegetables such as onions, carrots, and potatoes are excellent cooked in this manner.

ALL-PURPOSE STEW

Most people think of stew as being just that, stew, and nothing more. Or they think of it as a dish that accumulated. Not so! Stew can serve several purposes as a main dish, in pies; or it can be changed to make it into a rich soup. The three separate seasonings, beef, pork, and chicken, give it a most satisfying flavor.

To make approximately 50 servings

YOU WILL NEED

10 pounds lean beef, cubed
2 pounds lean pork, cubed
1 quart chicken broth
3 quarts hot water
2 pounds small, whole onions
3 pounds fresh carrots, peeled and chunked
3 pounds potatoes, peeled and chunked
1 pound chopped celery including some green tops
1 cup flour
1/2 cup butter
salt
black pepper

THE PREPARATION

Prepare the carrots, onions, potatoes, and celery ahead and set aside. In a large kettle bring the water and broth to a boil. Add 3 teaspoons salt and 1 teaspoon black pepper, then add the beef and pork, and reduce the heat to low. Cook slowly until the meats are almost tender. Add the onions, carrots, and celery and continue cooking until they are tender. Add the potatoes and let the mixture simmer for several minutes or until the potatoes are almost done. In a saucepan melt the butter and add the flour, stirring and cooking for about 5 minutes. Dip 4 or 5 cups broth from the mixture, and add, 1 cup at a time, to the butter and flour. Stir this until smooth, then add it slowly to the stew to thicken. Taste for seasonings. The stew ingredients should all be quite tender and still intact. The liquid should be the consistency of heavy cream. Serve in warm soup bowls.

VARIATION

For meat pies. Make the stew as given above and pour it into baking pans or casseroles, cover with regular pie pastry or with small biscuits. Bake in a hot oven, 425° until brown.

CHILI CON CARNE
Meat with chilis

The typical Mexican recipe for chili con carne is just that—or meat with seasonings. The seasonings are hot green peppers, chili powder, cumin, oregano, and sometimes coriander. The beans (frijoles, plain red beans, or pintos) are served as a side dish, and only occasionally cooked with the meats.

To make 25 generous servings

YOU WILL NEED

6 to 8 pounds lean beef, cut into small cubes or chunks
suet, a small piece
2 pounds fresh pork, cubed
1/2 cup pure lard, or bacon fat
1 cup onions, finely chopped
1 1/2 teaspoons oregano
1 teaspoon cumin powder
3 garlic cloves (optional)
8 to 10 tablespoons chili powder
4 tablespoons flour
2 tablespoons salt
water

THE PREPARATION

Instead of the usual grind of beef and pork ask the meat cutter to cut the meats into small cubes, or chunks. The meats retain a fuller flavor and also absorb the seasonings better when cut in this manner. Ask for a small piece of suet, about 1/4 pound. Blend the meats together and sprinkle with salt. Heat the fat and the suet to hot and add the meats. Cook, stirring occasionally, until the meats are slightly brown and all of the pink has disappeared. Add onions and all the seasonings except the chili powder. Combine the chili powder with the flour and sufficient water to make a paste. Add the paste to the meat and cook for about 15 minutes, slowly. Add sufficient water to cover the mixture generously. Reduce the heat to low, cover, and let simmer for about 40 minutes. Taste for salt. The chili seasonings require less salt than most other mixtures. Serve very hot with or without beans. Instead of serving with crackers, serve with Mexican spoon cornbread.

VARIATION

Add 4 cups chopped canned tomatoes, either to stretch the recipe or to please those who prefer a tomato flavor.

LASAGNE
Old-Style

I found this recipe almost by accident while on a tour through Italy. Our courier, who could speak excellent Italian, got it from the chef in a quaint little restaurant in Verona, Italy. I have adapted it, with minor changes, to fit our ingredients and for quantity cooking.

To make approximately 25 servings

YOU WILL NEED

1 1/2 pounds lasagne noodles, cooked according to package directions
4 pounds ground beef
1 pound country-style pork sausage
2 pounds cottage cheese, sieved
1 pound mozzarella cheese, thinly sliced
4 cups grated American cheese, or Parmesan

The sauce:
1/4 cup salad oil or olive oil
1 cup finely diced onion
2 quarts canned tomato sauce
1 pint canned tomato paste
1/4 cup finely chopped green peppers
1/4 cup finely chopped pimiento
1 1/2 teaspoon oregano
1 teaspoon thyme
2 bay leaves
1/8 teaspoon cayenne pepper
1 tablespoon salt

THE PREPARATION

Prepare the sauce first by heating the oil in a large heavy kettle or skillet. Sauté the onion, peppers, and pimiento until they are tender. Add all seasonings and tomato paste and sauce. Simmer the mixture, covered, for about 30 minutes.

Sprinkle the beef with salt, lightly, and combine with the sausage. Add to the sauce and simmer again for about 30 minutes or until the meat is quite tender and the mixture well-blended. Cook the noodles according to package directions. Drain them well and rinse with hot or cold water, depending on preference. In a large baking pan lay layers first of meat sauce, then noodles, then cheeses—first the cottage cheese, which has been well sieved, then the mozzarella, and then the grated American. Repeat the process until all ingredients are used. The grated cheese should come out on top. Bake at 350° for about 40 minutes, or until brown. Serve with a tossed salad, a light desert, and French bread to make a satisfying meal.

WIENERS SWEET and SOUR

A great many people think of this meat dish as being served only to young folks. Not so. Everyone likes a wiener now and then, depending of course, on the quality of the wieners. This dish is excellent served for a party refreshment, or as something very special for a church supper.

To make 25 servings of 2 wieners each

YOU WILL NEED
- 4 1/2 pounds wieners, with 12 count to a pound
- 2 6-ounce jars of prepared mustard
- 2 10-ounce jars of red currant jelly
- 1/4 cup lemon juice

THE PREPARATION

Cut the wieners diagonally into about three parts. In a large saucepan or heavy skillet, mix the mustard, jelly, and lemon juice together. Stir until blended. Add the wieners and heat slowly over low heat until the wieners are very hot and tender. Do not overcook. Shake the saucepan to make sure all the wieners are coated with the mixture. Let this mixture marinate for an hour or two and then reheat in order for the meat to be completely seasoned with the delightful sweet-and-sour flavor. Serve hot.

VARIATION I

Wieners with sauerkraut for 25 servings
4 1/2 pounds wieners
1 quart sauerkraut
2 cups grated sharp cheese

Split the wieners lengthwise down the center, but not quite through. Stuff with sauerkraut, sprinkle with cheese, and bake at 375° for about 25 minutes.

VARIATION II

Barbecued Wieners for 25 servings
4 1/2 pounds wieners
1 1/2 quarts barbecue sauce

Place wieners in baking pan, pour the sauce over them and bake at 375° for about 30 minutes, turning occasionally.

PORK

Although pork is not quite as universally eaten as beef and chicken, it is certainly one of the best of our meats for nutrition and satisfaction of flavor. When cooking pork it is well to remember that almost without exception, pork must be cooked well done.

Some cooking hints for pork

A cured ham, approximate weight 14 to 16 pounds, should bake or roast at 300° for about 4 hours. A fresh ham should cook almost twice that length of time.

Pork chops or pork steaks approximately 1 inch thick should cook for about 45 minutes or until quite tender and brown.

Pork spareribs approximately 2 to 3 pounds in weight should cook for about 1 1/2 hours.

Ham slices approximately 1/2 inch thick should cook for about 15 to 20 minutes each.

BAKED HAM with fruit glaze

To make approximately 50 servings

YOU WILL NEED

20 to 22 pounds whole ham
water, if needed

The glaze
1 cup brown sugar
1 cup whole Maraschino cherries
1/4 cup Maraschino cherry juice
2 tablespoons cornstarch
3 tablespoons whole cloves
2 teaspoons prepared mustard
1/4 cup lemon juice

THE PREPARATION

Trim the ham, cutting away a part of the heavy fat. Place in a preheated oven at 300° in a large roaster, on a baking rack, and add some water if preferred. Bake for about 4 1/2 to 5 hours. If boned or ready-to-eat ham is being used, shorten the time by about one-third. About 30 minutes before the ham has finished baking, remove it from the oven, drain well, and finish trimming as much of the skin and fat away as possible. Score the top side, then punch the cloves and cherries into the meat to make a design. Combine the glaze ingredients and spread them evenly over the ham. Return to the oven and increase the temperature to 425°. Bake until the ham is glazed and done. Test for tenderness by piercing with a sharp-pointed knife.

VARIATION

Baked ham with an orange glaze
Baked ham as given above

The glaze:
1 cup orange marmalade
1/2 cup brown sugar
2 tablespoons fresh lime juice
2 tablespoons cornstarch
1/3 cup pineapple juice

Follow the previous directions for glaze procedure

HAM LOAF
Congealed

To make approximately 25 servings (2 loaves)

YOU WILL NEED
- 2 1/2 quarts cooked, ground ham, with fat removed (about 6 pounds)
- 5 envelopes unflavored gelatin
- 1 cup cold water
- 6 cups chicken broth
- 3 tablespoons horseradish
- 3 tablespoons prepared mustard
- 1/2 cup mayonnaise
- 6 hard-cooked eggs, for garnish
- 1/2 cup pimiento strips, for garnish

THE PREPARATION

Prepare the ham, making sure it does not contain fat, gristle, or bone. (The loaf will not slice evenly unless it is free of these rough ingredients.) Dissolve the gelatin in the cold water. Bring the chicken stock to a boil, add the gelatin, and stir until smooth. Add all other ingredients except the eggs and pimiento. Pour into two loaf pans, about 9 1/2 x 5 x 3 inches, and refrigerate for several hours or overnight. A few hours before serving time, unmold the loaves onto serving platters. Separate the yolks from the whites of the hard-cooked eggs, which have been chilled, and press the whites of the eggs through a sieve over the entire top of each loaf. Then press the yolks over the white, leaving an edge all around the loaf to make a white border around a yellow fluffy mass. With care, use the pimiento strips to make a design over a part of the yellow. Chill again before serving. When ready to serve, cut with a sharp knife to make smooth, even slices. This is a very impressive entrée.

CREAMED HAM

To make this one of the most appreciated entrées, serve it over a square of Mexican spoon bread.

To make approximately 50 servings

YOU WILL NEED
- 6 to 7 pounds baked or boiled ham, cubed and fat removed
- 4 quarts milk
- 1 cup margarine or butter
- 1 cup flour
- salt, if needed
- 2 cups finely chopped celery
- 1 teaspoon white pepper
- 6 hard-cooked eggs
- 1/2 cup chopped pimiento

THE PREPARATION

Melt the butter and stir in the flour, cook and stir until blended. Add the milk gradually and cook over low heat, stirring constantly until the mixture is thick and smooth. Fold in the ham and all other ingredients, except the eggs. Cook over low heat for about 20 minutes, stirring occasionally. Just before serving, fold in the chopped eggs, and taste for seasonings. The ham will have made the mixture somewhat salty, therefore, salt with caution. Serve hot over Mexican spoon bread or over hot, crisp toast. Garnish with a small slice of pimiento and some hard-cooked egg or a sprig of parsley.

VARIATION

Curried ham for **50 servings**
- 6 to 7 pound ham, cooked and cubed
- 4 quarts milk
- 1 cup butter, melted
- 1 cup flour
- salt, if needed
- 1/2 cup minced celery
- 1/2 cup minced onion

4 tablespoons curry powder, added to melted butter
1 pound mushrooms, sliced
2 cups sour cream
1 teaspoon white pepper

Prepare according to directions for creamed ham.

STUFFED PORK CHOPS

To make approximately 50 servings

YOU WILL NEED

18 pounds pork chops (3 or 4 to a pound)
2 1/2 quarts milk
2 tablespoons salt
2 teaspoons black pepper

The stuffing:
4 1/2 pounds stale bread, cubed
2 1/2 quarts chicken or beef stock
salt to taste
2 tablespoons sage
1/3 cup grated onion
4 eggs
1/2 cup melted butter
dash of Tabasco sauce

THE PREPARATION

Prepare the stuffing first by combining all ingredients. Blend them lightly and set aside. Arrange the chops in baking pans in single layers. Sprinkle with salt and pepper, and bake in a preheated oven at 425° until slightly brown, turning as necessary to brown on both sides. With a sharp-pointed knife make a slash across each chop, and place a large tablespoonful or more of the stuffing over and into the slash. Pour the milk in and around the chops and return to the oven. Bake at 350° for about 1 hour, or until the milk has been almost absorbed and the chops are very tender. Serve hot, garnished with a sprig of parsley.

VARIATION I

Breaded pork chops for 50 servings
18 pounds pork chops, cut into 50 slices
2 1/2 cups bread crumbs
3 eggs, beaten
1 cup milk
2 tablespoons salt
1 teaspoon black pepper

Blend beaten eggs with milk. Dip chops in this mixture, then into bread crumbs. Place in well-greased baking pans, sprinkle lightly with salt and pepper. Brown quickly in hot oven 425° then reduce heat to 350° and bake for 1 hour, or until tender.

VARIATION II

Pork chops with pineapple slices for 50 servings
18 pounds pork chops, cut into 50 slices
2 No. 10 cans sliced pineapples, or 50 slices
2 tablespoons salt
1/2 cup soy sauce

Brown pork chops quickly in hot oven as given in stuffed pork chops recipe. Sprinkle lightly with salt, then lay a slice of pineapple on each chop. Sprinkle a few drops of soy sauce over the pineapple. Reduce heat to 350° and bake for 1 hour. Garnish with minced green peppers.

LAMB

Although lamb is not as universally eaten as beef, fish, pork, or chicken, it does have a following of people with discriminating tastes and it should be served as often as the budget and circumstances will allow.

The following suggestions are given to help the cooks in purchasing different cuts of lamb and a hint or two about the cooking procedure.

Roast leg-of-lamb. To make 50 servings, purchase 18 to 20 pounds of roast and cook at 300° from 30 to 35 minutes per pound for well done. The roast should be well trimmed at the market before it is weighed.

Ribs and chops. Purchase a total of 25 pounds for 50 servings, that is, allowing 2 chops for each serving. There should be about 4 chops per pound. Cook 1 1/2-inch thick chops about 16 to 18 minutes per pound for medium done, and 20 to 22 minutes per pound for well done.

Seasonings for lamb. Herbs are always recommended for lamb, and one of the most popular is mint. Other herbs and spices are: bay leaves; mustard; curry powder; garlic cloves; and marjoram.

CHICKEN

Next to beef no other meat is as universally eaten and enjoyed as chicken. There are countless methods of preparing and serving it, which adds to its popularity. It is one of the less-expensive proteins, and is most often recommended for persons who need a light and easily digested meat.

Some helpful hints for preparing chicken and fowl.

Broiling. Only tender young chickens, 2 1/2 pounds or under, should be broiled. Brush the chicken with some fat—either margarine, salad oil, or butter. Place under the broiler, but do not put too near the flame. Allow about 1 hour for cooking, turning the bird often and basting with the liquid that comes from the cooking.

Panfrying. The chicken is usually cut into serving pieces, seasoned with salt and pepper, dredged in flour or other seasonings, and browned in hot fat until crisp and tender. The fat should be about 1 to 1 1/2 inches deep. Turning and watching insures a delicate and satisfactory finish.

Deep-fat frying. I recommend this method when the institution owns a deep-fry appliance. The directions come with the equipment. The old method of standing over the stove to deep fry was tiring and exacting.

Stewing and simmering. Season the bird with about 2 teaspoons salt to each 4 pounds. Place in a large kettle that has a fitting lid. Cover with water and simmer for about 2 hours for each 4 to 5 pounds of fowl. The water should be kept at the simmering point, not boiling. This is the recommended method to use when the chicken is to be boned and skinned.

Roasting and baking chickens. Chickens are usually roasted uncovered in an oven at 325°, basted with the drippings or brushed with butter. Allow 3/4 to 1 pound fowl for each serving before roasting, and cook approximately 30 minutes per pound for a 5-pound chicken. Test for doneness by moving the drumstick—if it moves easily at the thigh joint, it should be done.

FRICASSEE OF CHICKEN

To make approximately 50 servings

YOU WILL NEED
- 12 chickens, about 2 1/2 pounds each, cut into quarters
- 3 quarts chicken stock
- 1 pound vegetable fat or butter
- 3 to 4 tablespoons salt
- 1 teaspoon black pepper
- 2 cups flour

For gravy:
1 cup fat
1 cup flour

THE PREPARATION

Prepare the chickens ahead by washing thoroughly. Pat dry with paper towels and cut into quarters. Add salt and pepper to the flour and dredge each piece in the mixture. Heat the shortening to hot, but not smoking. Brown the pieces quickly, turning and turning to brown evenly. Lay the pieces, as they come from the hot fat, in a baking pan. Make single layers when possible. When all pieces have been browned, add the gravy fat and flour to the remaining frying fat. Stir until smooth. Add the stock and stir again until smooth and well blended. Pour over the chicken and bake in a preheated oven at 350° for about 45 minutes or until the pieces are tender. Serve hot with some of the gravy for each serving.

CHICKEN TETRAZZINI

This delicious dish should be served as a one-dish meal, with only a fruit or vegetable salad, either French or rye bread, a drink, and a light dessert.

To make approximately 50 servings

YOU WILL NEED

5 pounds chicken, cooked, boned and cubed (about 18 pounds before cooking)
2 pounds spaghetti, cooked
1 quart chicken stock
3 quarts milk
1 pint light cream, or an equal amount of undiluted evaporated milk
4 cups mushrooms, sliced
1 cup pimientos, chopped
1/2 cup finely chopped onion
2 tablespoons salt
2 teaspoons white pepper
3 cups grated sharp cheese
1 cup butter or margarine
3/4 cup flour
parsley for garnish

THE PREPARATION

Prepare the chicken ahead and reserve the stock. Cook the spaghetti in some of the stock and set aside. Melt the margarine and sauté the onions. Add flour to the mixture and stir until well blended. Heat the milk and combine with the 1 quart of stock. Add the cream to this mixture and stir until smooth and blended. This should be a medium-thick sauce, the spaghetti will thicken it further. Fold in the mushrooms and pimiento, and combine with the boned chicken. Add the pepper and salt, adding the salt with caution—the stock and spaghetti will have been salted. In well-greased baking pans spread a layer of cooked spaghetti, then a layer of the chicken mixture, and continue the process until all of the ingredients have been used except the cheese. After all of the mixtures are spread evenly in layers, sprinkle the whole generously with the grated cheese. Bake at 425° for about 35 minutes or until the mixture is slightly brown and well set. It should come out thick enough to serve easily, that is, it should hold its shape when served. Sprinkle chopped fresh parsley over the servings for a nice garnish.

VARIATION

To make Turkey Tetrazzini, substitute the same amount of boned turkey for the chicken in the recipe, and follow the same preparation directions.

CREAMED CHICKEN

To make approximately 50 servings

YOU WILL NEED
- 5 to 6 pounds chicken, cooked, boned and cubed (about 18 pounds before cooking)
- 2 1/2 quarts chicken stock
- 2 1/2 quarts milk, hot
- 2 tablespoons salt
- 1 teaspoon white pepper
- 1 1/2 cups butter or margarine
- 2 cups flour

THE PREPARATION

Prepare the chicken ahead and reserve the stock. The stock will have been salted, so add more with caution. Melt the margarine or butter and stir in the flour, cook slowly for a few minutes, and gradually add the stock and milk. Stir until smooth and well blended. Add the pepper and cook slowly for about 10 minutes, stirring occasionally. Fold in the chicken pieces and heat again over low heat. Serve hot over either toasted English muffins, toast, or in pastry shells. A slice of hard-cooked egg with a small apple wedge resting on a lettuce leaf makes a beautiful garnish for this dish.

VARIATION

Curried Chicken, to serve 50
5 to 6 pounds cooked chicken, boned and cubed
4 1/2 quarts chicken stock and milk, combined
salt as needed
5 tablespoons curry powder
1 cup butter
1 1/2 cups flour
1 cup sour cream
2 cups sliced mushrooms

Follow preparation directions as given above and serve over steamed rice.

CHICKEN AND NOODLES

To make approximately 50 servings

YOU WILL NEED

5 to 6 pounds chicken, cooked, boned, and cubed (about 18 pounds before cooking)
2 1/2 pounds noodles, cooked
3 quarts milk, hot
4 1/2 quarts chicken stock
3/4 pound margarine or butter
3/4 cup flour
2 teaspoon white pepper
2 tablespoons salt
1/2 cup finely chopped onions
4 cups bread crumbs

THE PREPARATION

Prepare the chicken ahead and reserve the stock. The chicken stock will have been salted, therefore, add further salt with caution. Cook the noodles in some of the stock, add the pepper, and set aside. Melt the butter or margarine in a large heavy kettle, sauté the onions, then stir in the flour, and blend well. Gradually combine the stock, hot milk, chicken, and the butter mixture. Stir until blended. Cook over low heat for about 15 minutes, stirring occasionally. In greased baking pans spread the cooked noodles over the bottom, then the chicken mixture over the noodles. Continue adding and spreading the two separate mixtures until all ingredients are used. Sprinkle the tops with the bread crumbs and bake at 350° for about 30 minutes or until brown. Serve hot and with a sprinkle of chopped parsley as a garnish.

CHICKEN BREASTS ORIENTAL

To make 50 servings

YOU WILL NEED
- 50 chicken breasts of approx. 1/4 pound each
- 3 tablespoons salt
- 1 pound butter or margarine, for browning the breasts
- 3 6-ounce cans frozen orange juice, slightly diluted
- 1 pint orange marmalade
- sugar, if needed
- 1 cup butter, melted, for glaze mixture
- 1 teaspoon ginger
- 1/2 cup soy sauce
- rice (optional)

THE PREPARATION

Wash the chicken breasts thoroughly and pat dry with paper towels. Melt the margarine in baking pans and arrange the breasts in single layers in the hot fat, bone side down. Sprinkle lightly with salt. Brown quickly in a preheated oven at 425°, turning once or twice to brown evenly. After the breasts are brown, keep the bone side down for further cooking. Melt the cup of butter and add all other ingredients except rice. Mix well. Some sugar can be added at this point if needed. Taste to see. Baste the chicken with the orange mixture and bake at 350° until very tender and well glazed. A wedge of avocado, on a lettuce leaf, served with each breast makes a beautiful and an appealing entrée. It can be served with steamed rice, if desired.

VARIATION

Pineapple preserves and pineapple juice can be substituted for the orange mixture.

TURKEY
Roasted or Baked

When cooking turkeys allow about 18 minutes per pound for a 20-pound unstuffed bird; longer for stuffed. Test for doneness by moving the drumstick backward and forward. If it is loose and the meat shows no trace of blood, the turkey should be done.

To make 50 generous servings

YOU WILL NEED
- 2 20-pound turkeys (approximate weight)
- 3 or more tablespoons salt
- 2 teaspoons black pepper
- 1 pound margarine or butter
- 1/3 cup lemon juice
- water

THE PREPARATION

Wash the turkeys thoroughly, then rub them inside and out with a combination of melted margarine, lemon juice, salt, and pepper. Place them in a large roaster on a rack for roasting and without water. (If baking add 6 cups water with each turkey.) Place in a preheated oven at 425° and bake uncovered for about 45 minutes or until the bird is completely hot. Then reduce the heat, cover if baking, and complete the cooking at 325° for at least 18 minutes per pound. The turkeys should be quite tender by this time. Make the test for doneness. If the turkey breasts are brushed with butter toward the end of baking time and uncovered, and the heat raised to 425° again for a few minutes, the turkey will take on a beautiful brown glaze. Cool the turkeys about 30 minutes before slicing to keep the meat from breaking.

For quantity cooking it is more practical to bake the stuffing separately from the turkeys. Make 5 to 6 pounds of stuffing for each bird to serve 50 people.

Some suggestions for stuffing:

Plain bread stuffing. For 50 servings use 5 to 6 pounds dry bread, broken into small pieces; 2 1/2 to 3 quarts turkey stock; 5 eggs; 1 cup butter or turkey fat; seasonings such as chopped celery, 1/2 cup minced onion, sage, pepper, or other herbs. Mix, blend, and bake in well-greased baking pans separate from the turkeys, at 350° for about 45 minutes.

Sausage stuffing. Substitute 2 pounds sausage, well seasoned, for an equal amount of bread crumbs. Add 1 cup chopped celery, 1 cup minced green peppers, 6 eggs, salt, pepper and other herbs if desired. Mix, blend, and bake separate from the turkeys, at 350° for about 45 minutes.

Corn bread stuffing. This is a favorite in the South and Southwest. Substitute 4 to 5 pounds of corn bread crumbs for the plain bread. Bake as directed for bread stuffing.

Raisin and nut stuffing. Add 2 cups chopped pecans and 2 cups raisins to the plain bread stuffing.

SUGGESTIONS FOR MAKING USE OF TURKEY LEFTOVERS

The meat, bones, and carcass can be used in many ways. Boil the crushed carcass slowly in water to cover for about 3 hours. Season with herbs, onions, celery, parsley, tomatoes, etc. Strain and use for soups, white sauce, tomato sauce, or omit the tomatoes and use the broth for creamed meats. The leftover meats can be used for salads, creamed turkey, ground and highly seasoned for sandwiches, or made into a turkey loaf, following the recipe for meat loaf.

FISH

Cooking fish for a crowd is sometimes a chore for the person inexperienced in quantity cooking. However, it can be done with a certain amount of confidence if the fish menu is kept rather simple, and the purchasing done with care. The methods of preparing fish usually differ from community to community and the cook might take a cue from the tastes and wishes of the group in this regard.

Most markets have many types and kinds of fish ready to cook, even fillets that are breaded. The frozen and canned fish have labels that are well marked with purchasing information to assist the cooks.

An example of purchasing shellfish to serve 50: When buying headless shrimp, in shell, if the count is 12 to 16 per pound, and the cook plans to serve 6 per person, the amount to buy would be 25 pounds.

FISH FILLETS BAKED

To make 50 servings

YOU WILL NEED
- 15 pounds fish fillets, or steaks, cut into 50 slices
- 1 1/2 cups cornmeal
- 1 1/2 cups flour
- 2 tablespoons salt
- 1 teaspoon pepper
- 1/2 cup lemon juice
- 1 pound fat, bacon fat, or margarine, melted
- 1/2 cup milk combined with 1/2 cup water

THE PREPARATION

Combine the flour and cornmeal and set aside. Combine the salt, pepper, and lemon juice with the melted fat. Dip each fillet first in the fat mixture then in the flour and cornmeal. Place the fillets in a shallow baking pan, or pans, which have been greased and sprinkled with cornmeal. Lay the pieces close together in a single layer. Sprinkle lightly with the milk and water mixture and bake in a preheated oven at 450° for about 20 minutes or until lightly brown and tender. Serve with a small slice of lemon on each piece, and a sprinkle of paprika or chopped parsley.

BAKED TUNA

Because of its lightness this tuna dish is sometimes called a soufflé. It is not quite that, but its lightness, using separated eggs, makes it especially attractive for diet-conscious people.

To make approximately 50 servings

YOU WILL NEED
8 pounds tuna, flaked
1 quart milk
salt, if needed
1 teaspoon white pepper
12 eggs, separated
2 tablespoons grated fresh onion
2 cups bread crumbs
1/3 cup lemon juice

For the top:
1 1/2 quarts cheese sauce, see recipe p. 127

THE PREPARATION

Beat the egg yolks well, add onion and white pepper, and mix. Combine the bread crumbs with the milk and all other ingredients, except the egg whites. Combine with the tuna. Blend until smooth. Beat the egg whites until stiff, sprinkle with salt, and fold into the tuna mixture. Taste for salt and add only if needed.

167

Pour the mixture into greased baking pans gently to keep the mixture as fluffy as possible. Bake in a preheated oven at 375° for about 35 minutes or until the tuna is slightly brown and firm. Cut into squares and serve over a slice of hot toast, and top with 1 or 2 tablespoons of the cheese sauce. Garnish with a strip of pimiento or a crisp piece of parsley.

SALMON LOAF

To make approximately 50 servings (about 5 loaves)

YOU WILL NEED
- 8 pounds salmon, flaked
- 1 quart milk
- 6 cups bread crumbs
- 2 teaspoons salt
- 1/8 teaspoon Tabasco sauce
- 12 eggs, beaten
- 1/2 cup lemon juice
- 1/2 cup finely chopped green peppers
- pimiento strips for garnish

For top:
1 1/2 quarts cheese sauce, see recipe p. 127

THE PREPARATION

Scald the milk and pour over the bread crumbs and set aside. Separate the salmon with a fork in order for it to combine evenly with other ingredients. Beat the eggs and, with all other ingredients, combine with bread crumbs. Do not work the mixture any longer than is necessary to barely hold it together. The loaf becomes dense if worked too long. Form into 5 loaves, and place in greased loaf pans. Bake at 350° for about 35 minutes or until the loaves are firm and slightly brown. Serve hot with a cheese sauce and garnish with a strip of pimiento.

VEGETABLES

Some helps and hints for cooking a few of the more familiar and basic fresh vegetables using the boiling method. For approximately 50 servings of 1/2 cup each

Prepared vegetable	Ready-to-cook weight	Amount of boiling water	Cooking time in minutes
Asparagus spears	11 pounds	3 quarts	10-25
Beans, green	8 1/2 pounds	2 1/2 quarts	15-30
Beets, whole	13 pounds	to cover	35-40
Black-eyed peas	11 pounds	2 1/2 quarts	30-40
Broccoli spears	9 1/2 pounds	3 quarts	10-20
Cabbage, wedges or shredded	8 1/2 pounds	2 quarts	10-15
Carrots, whole & sliced	10 pounds	3 quarts	20-30
Cauliflower	8 pounds	4 1/2 quarts	15-20
Corn on cob	16-18 pounds	to cover	5-15
Eggplant, sliced	12 1/2 pounds	3 quarts	15-20
Okra	8 1/2 pounds	2 quarts	10-15
Onions, whole	14 pounds	6 quarts	25-30
Potatoes, small & whole	15-18 pounds	to cover	25-30
Spinach	12 pounds	2 cups, approx.	10-15
Squash, summer	14 pounds	2 quarts	10-20
Sweet potatoes for mashing	16-17 pounds	4 quarts	30-40
Turnips	14 pounds	3 quarts	15-20

To salt fresh vegetables. For each 1 quart of water the average amount of salt is 1 to 1 1/2 teaspoons, a little more for starchy vegetables.

Frozen vegetables. Ten pounds of frozen vegetables will make about 50 3-ounce portions. The labels on the frozen cartons should give clear directions as to number of servings and the cooking time. Cook uncovered, unless the package directions say otherwise. Salt as directed, or salt about 1 teaspoon for each quart of water. The vegetable should be served as soon as it is cooked. One pound of butter or margarine will season 50 portions. The extra liquid can be drained and frozen for later use.

Creamed vegetables. For 50 servings make 2 to 3 quarts of hot thin or medium white sauce, and pour over the vegetable at the last minute.

Canned vegetables. For 50 servings prepare two No. 10 cans. Drain off a part of the liquid, freeze for later use. Heat the vegetable in the remaining liquid and season with salt, pepper, and other appropriate seasonings. Serve the vegetable as it comes from the stove. Two No. 10 cans of vegetable are equal to approximately 26 cups or 6 1/2 quarts which makes 52 1/2-cup servings.

DRIED RED BEANS

To make approximately 50 generous servings

YOU WILL NEED
- 4 1/2 pounds dried red beans
- 2 to 3 gallons water
- 2 pounds salt pork, sliced
- 1 to 2 tablespoons salt
- 2 cups onions, sliced

THE PREPARATION

Wash and pick over the beans, and if time permits, soak them for several hours or overnight. In a large kettle bring the water to a boil, use the same water the beans were soaked in plus whatever additional amount is needed. Add the beans, salt pork, and onions. Cook slowly for 3 to 4 hours, or until the beans are quite tender. Taste for salt and add according to need. If extra water is needed during the cooking, add boiling water to keep the cooking temperature consistent.

VARIATION I

Ranch-style beans—for 50 servings
cooked red beans for 50
4 cups canned tomatoes
2 garlic cloves, minced
4 tablespoons chili powder
1/4 teaspoon cayenne pepper

VARIATION II

Chili beans with meat—for 50 servings
cooked red beans for 50
4 pounds ground beef, seasoned, and added 1 hour before beans are done
4 tablespoons chili powder
1 garlic clove, minced

VARIATION III

Fried-bean roll—for 50 servings
cooked red beans for 50
Cook the red beans as directed but continue cooking them long enough that they become almost dry. Cool, mash, and mold them into a round roll or rolls about 3 inches in diameter. Refrigerate for several hours, or until completely set. Cut into slices, about 1/2 inch thick, and fry in shallow hot bacon fat until slightly brown. This makes a delicious sandwich filling.

BAKED BEANS

A church supper, or a picnic, without a generous helping of freshly baked navy beans, well-seasoned and served hot, would be most unusual. This dish is always a welcome addition to a menu.

To make approximately 50 servings

YOU WILL NEED
- 5 pounds navy beans
- 2 to 2 1/2 gallons water
- 1 1/2 pounds salt pork, sliced
- 3 tablespoons salt
- 1 cup finely chopped onions
- 1 cup brown sugar
- 2 cups catsup
- 2 cups dark molasses
- 3 tablespoons prepared mustard
- 1/4 cup lemon juice

THE PREPARATION

Wash the beans carefully and soak them for several hours or overnight. Cook them in whatever water is needed in addition to the water they have been soaking in. Bring the beans to a boil and add the salt pork and onions and cook them for about 3 hours. Taste for salt and add only if needed. When the beans are almost tender, drain off all the liquid possible. Add all other ingredients and stir until well blended. Pour the mixture into greased baking pans and bake at 350° for about 1 1/2 to 2 hours, or until the beans are almost dry and well blended. Boston baked beans are placed in the oven before they are tender and baked for as long as it takes to get them blended into one tasty mass of flavors.

CREAMED CABBAGE

To make approximately 50 servings

YOU WILL NEED
- 10 pounds crisp, fresh cabbage, coarsely shredded
- 3 gallons water
- 3 tablespoons salt
- 3 quarts medium white sauce
- black pepper (optional)
- 1 cup finely chopped pimientos
- 3 cups bread crumbs

THE PREPARATION

Salt the water and bring to a boil. Add the cabbage and cook for about 10 minutes or until tender. Drain well and place in a buttered baking pan, or pans. Sprinkle with pepper, and spread the pimiento over the mixture. Pour the white sauce over cabbage slowly, allowing it to soak in as it is being poured. Over all this spread the bread crumbs and bake at 425° for about 20 minutes or until slightly brown and well blended. This mixture will not be firm but it should hold its shape somewhat. The pimientos will come to the top in little amounts to make a slight garnish.

VARIATION

Cabbage au gratin for 50 servings
10 pounds shredded cabbage cooked as directed above
3 quarts medium white sauce
1/2 cup finely chopped onion
1/2 cup finely chopped green peppers
1 quart grated sharp cheese
Follow preparation and baking directions as given above.

SWEET & SOUR RED CABBAGE

This dish is usually served with sauerbraten but it goes just as well with many other meats. Try it with a pot roast or with pork chops.

To make approximately 25 servings

YOU WILL NEED
2 large heads of red cabbage
10 slices breakfast bacon, chopped
1 cup finely chopped onions
3 tart cooking apples, cored and sliced
1 cup white vinegar combined with 1 cup water
1 1/2 cups brown sugar
salt
black pepper

THE PREPARATION

Remove the outer leaves and hard core from the cabbage, wash it thoroughly and shred coarsely. In a large heavy kettle, with fitting lid, cook the bacon and onion until both are tender. Add the cabbage, pressing it down as it is being added. Sprinkle with salt and pepper (about 2 teaspoons salt and 1 teaspoon black pepper). Combine the vinegar and water and pour over the cabbage. Cover the whole with the brown sugar and sliced apples, spreading both evenly. Cover with a heavy lid, reduce the heat to slow, and cook for about 1 1/2 hours or until the mixture is completely tender and blended into one purple mass.

CORN PUDDING

To make approximately 50 servings

YOU WILL NEED
- 2 No. 10 cans corn, cream style
- 3 quarts milk
- 1/2 cup sugar
- 2 tablespoons salt
- 1 cup flour
- 1/2 cup margarine or butter
- 4 tablespoons grated onion
- 12 eggs, beaten
- 1 cup finely chopped pimiento
- 1 cup parsley

THE PREPARATION

In a heavy, large kettle, melt the butter or margarine, and stir in the flour. Cook and stir until smooth. Gradually pour in the milk, then the corn, and stir again until the mixture is well blended. Beat the eggs, and add sugar, salt, onion, and pimiento. Slowly combine the two mixtures. Pour into buttered baking pans, sprinkle with parsley and bake in a preheated oven at 325° for about 40 minutes or until the pudding is slightly brown and well set.

BUTTERED CARROTS

To make approximately 50 servings

YOU WILL NEED
- 10 to 12 pounds fresh carrots
- 3 quarts water
- 1 tablespoon salt
- 1 cup butter or margarine, melted
- 1/2 cup sugar

THE PREPARATION

Wash the carrots thoroughly, trim the ends and blemishes. Bring the water to a boil, add salt, and drop in the carrots. Cover and cook for about 30 minutes or until tender. Remove from the liquid, cool, skin and split lengthwise into uniform slices. Put in a baking dish and sprinkle the sugar over them, then pour the melted butter over all. Bake in a hot oven, 425°, for about 20 minutes. Chopped parsley makes an appetizing finish to this simple dish.

VARIATION

To make carrots with orange sauce. Follow the directions above for cooking the carrots, and pour over them a mixture of 1 cup frozen orange juice undiluted, 1 cup melted butter, 1 cup sugar, and 4 tablespoons cornstarch dissolved in 1 cup water. Bake in 375° oven for about 30 minutes, until the carrots take on a glaze.

MASHED POTATOES

To make approximately 50 servings

YOU WILL NEED
- 15 to 18 pounds potatoes
- 2 tablespoons salt
- 2 teaspoons white pepper
- 4 cups undiluted evaporated milk
- 6 cups liquid from potatoes
- 1/2 cup butter
- water to cover

THE PREPARATION

Peel the potatoes, cut into halves or quarters.
Bring the water to a boil, add salt and potatoes. Cover and cook until quite tender, about 30 minutes. Drain them well, reserving the liquid. Mash, either with electric mixer or by hand, add the milk, butter, and sufficient liquid from the potatoes to bring the mixture to the desired thickness. They should be a fluffy, light mass. Sprinkle with the pepper, if desired. Keep warm by placing the kettle in a large pan of hot water.

POTATOES AU GRATIN

To make approximately 50 servings

YOU WILL NEED
- 12 to 13 pounds potatoes
- 2 tablespoons salt
- 1 teaspoon black pepper
- 1 1/2 quarts white sauce
- 3/4 cup mayonnaise
- 3 to 4 cups bread crumbs

THE PREPARATION

Boil the potatoes in water to cover, with jackets on, until barely tender. Remove from the hot water and cool. Peel, or skin, and slice. Place the slices in buttered baking pans, spreading out to keep the layers even. Sprinkle with salt and pepper. Blend the mayonnaise with the white sauce and pour the mixture over the potatoes. Sprinkle generously with the bread crumbs, and bake at 375° for about 30 minutes or until brown and the potatoes have absorbed the sauce. Serve hot with chopped parsley for a garnish.

SWEET POTATO PUFFS

When these are served in individual puffs, that is, dished up in a large helping which stands alone, with a bit of finely chopped almonds sprinkled over the top of each, they make a very special addition to any meal.

To make approximately 50 servings

YOU WILL NEED

14 to 16 pounds sweet potatoes
water to cover
2 tablespoons salt
1 cup brown sugar
8 eggs, separated
1 cup butter
1/2 teaspoon nutmeg
1 teaspoon cinnamon
1 cup toasted shredded almonds for garnish

THE PREPARATION

Peel the potatoes and cut into large pieces. Drop into salted, boiling water to barely cover. Reduce the heat and cook slowly until very tender, about 30 minutes. Lift the potatoes out of the liquid, make sure they are well drained. Mash them until they are smooth and fluffy. Stir in the egg yolks, the sugar, butter, and seasonings. Stir or beat again until fluffy. Whip the egg whites until stiff, and fold them into the potato mixture carefully. Pour into greased baking pans and bake at 375° until the mixture is slightly brown and puffed. Serve by spooning the potatoes up in individual heaps of about 1/2 cup each, and sprinkle with almonds. Delicious.

YELLOW SQUASH

To make approximately 50 servings

YOU WILL NEED

12 to 14 pounds yellow summer squash
2 quarts chicken broth
salt, if needed
1/2 cup margarine
10 slices breakfast bacon, chopped

THE PREPARATION

Prepare the squash by scrubbing and peeling lightly with a potato peeler. If the squash is not small, young, and tender, cut it away from the seeds. Do not use any seeds that are large or tough. Bring the broth to a boil, add the bacon and squash, and salt if needed. The broth and the bacon will add salt, therefore, salt with caution. Cook uncovered for about 20 minutes, toss the squash occasionally to insure even cooking. Add the butter and, when the squash is tender but not overcooked, lift it from the liquid with a slotted spoon and serve hot. For a colorful garnish sprinkle the servings with crisp, shredded green peppers.

VARIATION

Yellow squash Mexican style
12 pounds yellow squash, cooked as above
2 cups finely chopped onions
1 quart canned tomatoes, chopped and drained
6 tablespoons chili powder
1 quart grated sharp cheese

Combine all ingredients, except cheese. Cook until tender. Drain excess liquid. Pour into greased baking pans. Spread with cheese and bake for about 45 minutes at 350° or until slightly brown and almost dry.

ZUCCHINI SQUASH PARMESAN

To make approximately 50 servings

YOU WILL NEED
12 to 14 pounds zucchini squash, uniform size
2 1/2 quarts water, or a little more
1 tablespoon salt
1 cup butter, melted
2 1/2 cups Parmesan cheese, grated
1 1/2 teaspoons oregano
paprika

THE PREPARATION

Select the squash with care; it should be young, tender, and of uniform size. Scrub it thoroughly, trim off ends and all blemishes. Slice lengthwise in half. Bring the water to a boil, add salt and the squash. Reduce the heat and cook slowly for about 10 minutes, or until almost tender. Remove from liquid with a slotted spoon and lay in a greased baking pan, or pans, cut-side up. Pour the melted butter over the halves, then sprinkle with the oregano and then the paprika. Shake the pan to distribute the seasonings, then add the cheese by spreading carefully over each halve. Bake at 425° until the cheese is melted. Serve at once.

VARIATION

Zucchini with tomatoes and onions to serve 50
12 to 14 pounds tender, young zucchini, cooked in salty water until almost tender and drained
1 quart canned tomatoes, drained and chopped
1/2 cup margarine
1 cup chopped onions, sautéed in margarine until tender
2 tablespoons sugar
1 teaspoon black pepper

Combine and cook again for about 10 minutes. Lift out of liquid to serve.

BAKED EGGPLANT

To make approximately 50 servings

YOU WILL NEED

12 to 13 pounds fresh eggplant
1 tablespoon salt
2 1/2 quarts water
1 quart beef stock
10 eggs
1/2 cup mayonnaise
1/2 cup butter
1/2 cup finely chopped onion
1 cup finely chopped celery
3 cups milks
1 cup flour
2 tablespoons minced canned green chili peppers
4 cups bread crumbs

THE PREPARATION

Peel the eggplant, slice crosswise, about 1 inch thick, and remove a portion of the seeds. In sufficient water to barely cover, about 2 1/2 quarts, add 1 tablespoon salt and the eggplant. Cook only until tender, about 10 or 15 minutes. With a slotted spoon remove the eggplant to a shallow pan to cool. The liquid can be frozen and used later. Bring the beef stock to a boil, drop in the celery, onion, and chili peppers, and cook slowly until tender. If the stock shrinks, add 2 cups of the liquid retained from eggplant. In a large saucepan melt the butter and stir in the flour. Stir in the mayonnaise gradually until completely smooth. Gradually add the milk and stir until blended. In a large mixing bowl beat the eggs until light and slightly thick, then combine all of the mixtures together except the bread crumbs. Taste for seasoning and correct if needed.

Pour the mixture into buttered baking pans and bake in a preheated oven at 350° for about 35 minutes or until brown and firm. Garnish with slices of crisp, green peppers.

STEWED TOMATOES Old-Style

To make approximately 50 servings

YOU WILL NEED
- 2 No 10 cans tomatoes
- 1 cup finely chopped onions
- 2 tablespoons salt
- 1 teaspoon black pepper
- 1/2 cup sugar
- 1/2 cup bacon fat
- 1 loaf pullman-size bread

THE PREPARATION

Heat the tomatoes in a large kettle, add onions, salt, pepper, sugar, and fat. Cook slowly for about 15 minutes, or until the onions are tender and the mixture blended. Cut the bread into slices, then into squares. Add to the tomatoes and reduce the heat. Simmer for about 15 minutes. The mixture should be thick enough to serve without being soupy. If necessary drain some of the liquid off. Taste for seasonings and correct as needed. Serve hot.

BAKED TOMATOES

To make 50 servings

YOU WILL NEED
50 ripe tomatoes, medium size
salt
sugar
1 1/2 cups minced onions
2 to 3 cups bread crumbs

THE PREPARATION

Wash the tomatoes and cut a cone-shaped piece from the center of each. Sprinkle first a little salt, then a little sugar, and next some of the minced onion into the center of each tomato. Place in buttered baking pans and add about 1 teaspoon bread crumbs to the top of each. Bake at 425° for about 20 minutes or until the tomatoes are tender. Serve hot with a garnish of chopped parsley over the tops.

VARIATION

Omit bread crumbs and add 1 teaspoon minced mushrooms to the top of each tomato. Cook as directed above.

PASTA

MACARONI, SPAGHETTI, AND NOODLES

To make approximately 50 servings of 1/2 cup each, when serving with sauce, cook 4 pounds macaroni, spaghetti, or noodles in about 3 gallons boiling water with 3 to 4 tablespoons salt. To keep the mixture from boiling over, add 4 or 5 tablespoons cooking oil to the boiling water. Cook for about 15 minutes unless the package label calls for another cooking time. When done, lift the pasta out of the liquid with a slotted spoon, or rinse in hot or cold water, or don't rinse, as desired. A sauce can be served over the pasta, or it can be served with buttered bread crumbs and a little extra butter.

MACARONI AND CHEESE

To make approximately 50 servings

YOU WILL NEED

3 pounds macaroni
2 1/2 gallons boiling water
3 tablespoons salt
1/2 cup margarine

The sauce:
2 pounds grated cheese
1 pound butter or margarine
1 1/2 cups flour
2 teaspoons salt
2 1/2 quarts milk, hot
1 teaspoon white pepper
1 cup mayonnaise

THE PREPARATION

Cook the macaroni according to directions on package, or for cooking pasta as given in this section. Drain or not, as desired. Pour into two large baking pans and add the sauce, spreading it well over the macaroni.

To make the sauce. Melt the butter or margarine, and stir in the flour. Cook and stir until smooth and blended. Add the mayonnaise, pepper, and salt and stir again. Add the hot milk gradually, stirring constantly. When smooth and slightly thick, pour over the macaroni. Shake the pans to distribute the ingredients evenly. Sprinkle the tops generously with the cheese and bake in a preheated oven at 350° for about 30 minutes or until brown and almost dry.

GRITS SOUFFLÉ

This dish makes a wonderful base for creamed chicken or other creamed meat. It can also be served as a part of a Mexican or Spanish menu as the hot bread.

To make approximately 25 servings

YOU WILL NEED
- 4 cups hominy grits
- 6 eggs
- 1 cup butter or margarine
- salt
- 2 cups grated sharp cheese
- 4 tablespoons minced Jalapeño peppers, more or less

THE PREPARATION

Cook grits according to package directions, and salt as directed or according to taste. Just before removing the grits from heat add all other ingredients. Stir and beat until the mixture is completely blended. It will become quite thick while it is being beaten. Pour into well buttered casseroles, or baking pans, and bake at 400° for about 30 minutes or until slightly brown. Cut into squares or slices, and serve very hot. Delicious.

BAKED RICE
a basic recipe

If the rice is purchased in bulk, use 2 cups water for 1 cup rice, and 1 teaspoon salt for each quart of water. A simple rice dish can be served with countless meat entrees, such as steaks, chicken, beef, turkey, and so on. The cook can usually follow the cooking directions on the package and be quite sure of results.

To make approximately 50 servings

YOU WILL NEED
3 pounds rice
2 quarts consommé
2 cups pecan meats
2 cups ripe olives, thinly sliced
1/2 cup margarine or butter

THE PREPARATION

Prepare the rice according to package directions, or follow the directions given above. The cooked rice should be fluffy and slightly dry. Add the other ingredients and bake in well-buttered baking pans for about 35 minutes at 350° or until the top is slightly brown and the rice almost dry. If the mixture appears a little too moist before baking, sprinkle the top with 1 or 2 cups cracker crumbs.

VARIATION

Curried rice to serve 50
3 pounds rice, cooked according to package directions
1/2 cup butter
1 cup finely chopped onions, sautéed in the butter
2 quarts chicken stock
4 tablespoons curry powder, heated with sautéed onions
1/2 cup flour, added to stock after first making a paste with 1/2 cup water, and stirring and cooking until thick

Combine all ingredients and bake for 30 minutes at 350°.

SPANISH RICE

I have served this delicious starch dish at parties, church suppers, luncheons, and even brunches. It is a popular dish and very tasty.

To make approximately 50 servings

YOU WILL NEED
4 pounds rice
2 quarts canned tomatoes, chopped fine
2 cups finely chopped onions
3/4 cup bacon fat
6 tablespoons chili powder
salt, if needed
1/2 teaspoon cayenne pepper

THE PREPARATION

Cook the rice according to package directions and salt accordingly. A little more salt may be needed when the onions and tomatoes are added. Taste before adding extra salt. After the rice has cooked, keep it hot while preparing the remainder of the dish. In a large, heavy kettle, melt the bacon fat and sauté the onions until tender. Add the seasonings and stir until smooth. Add the tomatoes and blend. Combine the mixture with the rice, folding it in in order to keep the rice from becoming a mush. Cook again over very low heat, stirring occasionally to keep from sticking. It should be almost dry after cooking, but moist enough to have a full flavor. Serve very hot on large warm platters. Garnish with thin rings of fresh green peppers.

> You must reflect carefully beforehand with whom you are to eat and drink, rather than what you are to eat and drink. For a dinner of meats without the company of a friend is like the life of a lion or a wolf.
> —Epicurus

DESSERTS

You will find a number of recipes in this section for small amounts. Many of the best desserts have a better quality when made for a small number at a time, rather than doubling or tripling a recipe. Of course, it will be left up to the cook, but I suggest that, when in doubt, repeat the recipe.

Suggestions for last minute desserts. On occasion the cooks will need to put together some sweet, or something to replace a sweet, on short notice. Here are a few combinations that I have used in such emergencies.

1. Angel food cake with canned fruit. Slice a wedge of commercial angel food, pour about 1/4 cup canned fruit juice over it, and lay a a few slices or chunks of the fruit on that. Whipped cream can be added if desired.
2. Serve a small bowl of vanilla ice cream with a tablespoon of lemon or chocolate custard over it.
3. In a sherbet glass serve a dessert of canned or fresh fruit with a base of crumbled vanilla wafers in the bottom of the glass and over the top of the fruit.

4. Slices of sharp or mild cheddar cheese with a wedge of raw apple served on individual dessert plates.
5. A fresh fruit of some kind, about 3-ounces, and about 2 tablespoons of creamed cheese, softened with sour cream and sweetened.

PIES AND COBBLERS

Pie crust should be tender, short, flaky, and a delicate brown. In making the crust the ingredients should be combined with as little handling as possible. Rolling the crust out needs to be done with only a little flour, just enough to keep it manageable. The crust can be made in advance, wrapped in waxed paper and stored in the refrigerator to be used as needed. Eight 8-inch pies will make 50 servings.

Cobblers are made in large amounts, usually with canned or fresh fruits and the regular crust rolled out to cover the total amount, or rolled out and cut in squares or strips and either placed just over the top, or placed under and over the fruits. Another crust used for cobblers is made with milk, butter, flour, sugar, and baking powder. This is blended into a smooth batter and poured on the bottom of the baking pan with the fruit placed on top of this. The dough rises to the top and makes a double crust.

PIE CRUST

To make double crusts for 8 8-inch pies

YOU WILL NEED
3 quarts all-purpose flour
3 1/2 tablespoons salt
5 1/2 cups shortening
1 1/2 cups water approximately
flour for rolling

THE PREPARATION

Sift the flour and salt together and work in the shortening until it resembles cornmeal. Add the water gradually and mix the dough just enough to pull it together. Form it into a ball and let it rest for 20 minutes, or chill for an hour or so before using.

GRAHAM CRACKER CRUMB CRUSTS

To make single pie crusts for 8 8-inch pies

YOU WILL NEED
4 quarts graham cracker crumbs
1 1/2 cups sugar
3 cups butter or margarine, melted

THE PREPARATION

Add the sugar to the crumbs and mix well. Reserve 1 cup or more, if needed, to sprinkle over tops of pies later. Work the butter into the crumbs until the mixture will hold its shape when pressed into pie pans. Press the mixture firmly on the bottom of pans and build it up on the sides. Another pie pan may be set on the crust to help hold the shape. Chill well before using, or bake at 350° for about 10 minutes.

VARIATION

Vanilla Wafer crust. Use the amounts given above and substitute vanilla wafer crumbs for the graham cracker. This makes a more delicate crust than the graham cracker crumbs, and the flavor is not quite as strong as the crackers.

CHEESE PASTRY

Use this pastry to make small turnovers filled with a tart fruit filling, or use it for a delicate meat filling and serve as an entrée. It can also be made tiny and served with a meat filling for an appetizer.

To make about 2 dozen small turnovers

YOU WILL NEED
- 1/2 cup butter or margarine
- 1 cup grated sharp cheese
- 2 cups all-purpose flour
- 4 tablespoons water
- salt

THE PREPARATION

Mix all ingredients together, using just enough water to make a dough thick enough to roll out. If using for meat pastry, add 1/4 teaspoon salt. Roll out about 1/4 inch thick, cut into rounds 3 inches in diameter. Place 1 tablespoon of filling on the round and fold over. Secure edges with a fork. Prick the top of the round with a fork and place on a baking sheet. Bake at 350° about 20 minutes or until brown.

COCONUT CRUST

This fragile pie shell can be filled with a cream filling, custards, or a chiffon. It can also be the base for a whipped cream-and-fruit mixture.

To make a single crust for 1 8-inch pie

YOU WILL NEED
- 1 1/2 cups flaky coconut
- 3 tablespoons melted sweet butter
- 1/2 cup granulated sugar, or 3/4 cup powdered sugar

THE PREPARATION

Combine the ingredients and mix until well blended. Add more sugar or more melted butter if necessary to hold the coconut together. Press evenly over the bottom and sides of a well-buttered 8-inch pie pan. Chill until firm and well set.

MERINGUE SHELLS

To make 50 small individual shells

YOU WILL NEED
- 3 cups egg whites—about 28 eggs
- 1 1/2 teaspoon salt
- 2 teaspoons cream of tartar
- 6 cups sugar

THE PREPARATION

Add salt and cream of tartar to the egg whites and beat them until very frothy. Start adding the sugar, about 1/4 cup at a time, beating well after each addition, until the sugar is all used. Beat until the whites hold a firm shape, about 20 minutes. Place on well-greased and floured baking sheets and form them into nests, building the sides up to hold a mixture that might be placed in them. Bake 1 hour at 275°. They should be slightly brown and dry. Excellent to use for serving ice creams, custards, or fruits with whipped cream.

MERINGUE SHELL

To make a single pie shell for 1 9-inch pie

YOU WILL NEED
- 3 egg whites
- 1/4 teaspoon cream of tartar
- pinch of salt
- 3/4 cup sugar
- 1 teaspoon vanilla

THE PREPARATION

Add the salt and cream of tartar to the egg whites and beat them until frothy. Start adding the sugar, little by little, and beat after each addition until they are stiff enough to hold a firm shape, about 10 minutes. Fold in the vanilla. Spoon into a buttered 9-inch pie pan, and shape by building up the sides. Bake at 275° for about 1 hour. This is the perfect shell for an angel filling or for chiffons, also for a whipped cream-and-fruit mixture.

CRUST FOR COBBLERS

To make a crust for two large cobblers

YOU WILL NEED
- 2 quarts all-purpose flour
- 3 tablespoons baking powder
- 2 teaspoons salt
- 1 1/2 cups margarine or butter
- 2 1/2 cups milk, approximately

THE PREPARATION

Sift the flour, baking powder, and salt together and blend in the butter or margarine with a fork or with the fingers, until it resembles cornmeal. Add the milk and pull the mixture together into a ball. Divide into two equal portions, or divide according to number of pans being used. Roll out each portion to fit the pan, place carefully over the fruit. Brush with milk, or with a mixture of beaten egg and 1 tablespoon of water. Sprinkle the top with sugar and bake at 400° for about 30 minutes or until brown.

VARIATION

To make a pouring batter. Follow the recipe above but increase the milk to 6 cups and add 3/4 cup sugar. Blend all ingredients together into a thick pouring batter. More milk may be needed. Pour the batter in the bottoms of buttered pans and add the fruit to the top. Bake at 425° for the first 15 minutes, then reduce the heat to 375° and bake for another 20 or 30 minutes or until the pastry comes to the top of the fruit and is brown.

Let the stoics say what they please, we do not eat for the good of living, but because the meat is savory and the appetite is keen.

—Emerson

ANGEL CHOCOLATE PIE

To make one 9-inch pie to serve 8

YOU WILL NEED
- 1 cup semisweet chocolate pieces
- 1/4 cup hot strong coffee
- 1 teaspoon vanilla, or rum flavoring
- sprinkle of salt
- 1 cup heavy cream, whipped

Crust:
Use either meringue shell or coconut crust for one pie

THE PREPARATION

Add the chocolate pieces to the hot coffee and dissolve them over hot water in a double boiler. Stir until smooth. Add a sprinkle of salt and cool. Whip the cream to a stiff peak, fold in the flavoring and the chocolate mixture. Pour into whatever pie shell is desired and chill for several hours or overnight before serving. A garnish of shredded chocolate makes a beautiful finish.

CHOCOLATE PIE

To make filling for 8 8-inch pies

YOU WILL NEED
- 3 1/2 quarts milk
- 1 quart half-and-half cream, or an equal amount of undiluted evaporated milk
- 5 1/2 cups sugar
- 2 cups cocoa
- 1 cup flour
- 1 1/2 cups cornstarch
- 16 eggs, separated
- 1 teaspoon salt
- 2 tablespoons vanilla
- 8 8-inch baked pie shells

THE PREPARATION

Combine the flour, cocoa, cornstarch, and 4 1/2 cups of sugar. Stir until well blended. Add this mixture to the cream and stir until smooth. Heat the milk over hot water, to hot not boiling, and stir in the first mixture. Cook slowly, stirring constantly, until the mixture is thick. Beat the egg yolks until creamy, add the other cup of sugar to them, then beat again slightly. Add slowly to the thickened custard and stir gently until blended. Cook over low heat again for about 5 minutes, stirring. Add the salt and vanilla, and cool slightly before filling the pie shells. Divide the mixture into 8 equal parts and spoon into the shells, piling the custard a little higher in the center than at the edges. If covering with a meringue, beat the whites until stiff, sweeten with another 1 cup of sugar, spread on the pies and bake at 425° until brown, about 10 minutes. Chill before serving. Or whip 1 1/2 quarts of heavy cream, sweeten it slightly, and spread over the pies instead of the meringue, and garnish with shredded unsweetened chocolate.

LEMON CHESS PIE

To make 1 9-inch pie (to serve 25 people make three of these pies)

YOU WILL NEED
- 4 eggs
- 1 cup sugar
- 1/2 cup white Karo syrup
- 1 tablespoon flour
- 1 tablespoon cornmeal
- 1/3 cup lemon juice
- 1 tablespoon grated lemon rind
- 4 tablespoons light cream
- 1 9-inch unbaked pie shell

THE PREPARATION

Prepare the unbaked pie shell ahead. Beat the eggs until slightly thick and creamy. Add the sugar and syrup and blend. Stir the flour and cornmeal together and add to egg mixture. Mix well. Add lemon juice, rind, and the cream. Beat or stir the mixture until smooth and well blended. Pour into the unbaked pie shell and bake for 15 minutes at 425°, then reduce the heat to

350° and bake for another 25 minutes or until the pie is well set.

DUTCH APPLE PIE

Although this pie is not considered the truly great American apple pie, it is certainly delicious. It is especially good served hot with a dollop of sour cream on each piece. Each pie in this recipe will serve 6 persons.

To make 8 8-inch pies

YOU WILL NEED
- 12 to 15 pounds fresh, tart cooking apples (about 9 quarts peeled and sliced)
- 6 to 8 cups sugar, depending on tartness of apples
- 1 1/2 cups all-purpose flour
- 1/2 teaspoon salt
- 2 teaspoons cinnamon
- 1 teaspoon nutmeg
- 2 1/2 cups half-and-half cream
- 1 cup milk, or a little more
- pastry for 8 pies, double crust

THE PREPARATION

Prepare the pastry ahead and have the bottom shell of the pies in place. A lattice or plain crust can be used for the top, depending on preference. Peel and slice the apples, place about 4 1/2 cups on the bottom pie crust. Blend the flour, salt, sugar, spices, cream, and milk together. Stir or beat until the mixture is smooth and entirely blended. Pour about 1 cup of the cream mixture over the apples. Add the top crust, brush it with milk, and bake at 425° for about 15 minutes, then reduce the heat to 350° and continue to bake for about 40 minutes, or until the pie is brown and the apples quite tender. With a sharp, pointed knife, test to make sure the apples are done.

OLD-FASHIONED BUTTERMILK PIE

To make 1 8-inch pie (to serve 25 people make three of these pies)

YOU WILL NEED
- 3 eggs
- 1 cup fresh buttermilk
- 1 teaspoon vanilla
- 1 1/3 cups sugar
- 3 tablespoons flour
- 1/4 cup sweet cream butter, melted
- 1 tablespoon cornmeal
- 1 8-inch unbaked pie shell

THE PREPARATION

Prepare the unbaked pie shell ahead. Beat the eggs, add buttermilk and flavoring. Combine with the sugar, flour, and cornmeal and beat until smooth. Fold in the melted butter and stir again. Pour into the unbaked pie shell and bake at 350° for about 35 minutes, or until the pie is well set. The cornmeal forms a mealy crust over the top of the pie and helps with the browning of the custard. This is a tart, rich, and delicious pie.

PUMPKIN PIE
Thanksgiving-style

To make 8 8-inch pies

YOU WILL NEED
- 3 No. 2 1/2 cans pumpkin (or 2 1/2 quarts)
- 16 eggs
- 2 cups brown sugar
- 3 1/2 cups white sugar
- 3 quarts milk with 1 13-ounce can of evaporated milk as a part of this amount
- 2 teaspoons salt
- 1 teaspoon nutmeg
- 2 teaspoons cinnamon
- 1/2 teaspoon cloves
- 1 teaspoon allspice
- 1/2 cup flour
- pastry for 8 unbaked pie shells

THE PREPARATION

Prepare unbaked pie shells ahead. In a large saucepan combine all of the spices with the sugars, add the pumpkin and cook over low heat until the mixture is thoroughly blended, about 10 minutes. Beat the eggs, add milk, salt, and flour. Beat and stir until smooth. Combine the two mixtures and stir again until blended. To avoid spilling the mixture as it is being placed in the oven, partially fill the shells and set in the oven before completing the filling. Bake in a preheated 400° oven for about 1 hour or until the crust is brown and the custard is well set. Test for doneness by piercing the center of a pie with a pointed knife. If it comes out clean, the pie is done.

COBBLERS

CHERRY COBBLER

Although this recipe is for canned fruit, frozen or fresh may be used just as well. The sweetening is determined by the fruit being used. When making cobblers with frozen fruits be sure to read the labels carefully, to learn the sugar content of the package. Fresh fruits are always sweetened according to their tartness. The sugar measurement in this recipe can be used as an estimate for other fruits.

To make approximately 50 servings

YOU WILL NEED

4 quarts canned pie cherries, or 1 1/3 No. 10 cans, water packed and drained
3 to 4 cups sugar, depending on tartness of cherries
1 cup cornstarch
2 quarts cherry juice, drained from canned fruit
1/2 cup margarine or butter
1 teaspoon salt

Pastry:
1/2 recipe for regular pie pastry, or the cobbler crust recipe

THE PREPARATION

Drain the cherries and add some water to the juice if necessary to equal 2 quarts of liquid. Bring the juice to a boil. Blend the cornstarch, sugar, and salt together and add to the boiling juice, little by little, stirring constantly. Reduce the heat and cook, stirring, until the mixture is transparent and slightly thick, about 10 minutes. Stir in the butter and cherries. Taste for sweetness and correct according to need. Pour the mixture into one or two large, well-buttered, baking pans, and cover with whatever pastry is to be used. Brush the pastry with milk and bake in a preheated oven at 400° for about 30 minutes or until brown.

VARIATION

Follow these same directions for other fruit cobblers, using such fruits as apples, blueberries, peaches, blackberries, and so on.

APRICOT COBBLER
Canned fruit

To make approximately 50 servings

YOU WILL NEED

1 1/2 No. 10 cans apricots, water packed, drained
1 1/2 quarts apricot juice
1 cup cornstarch
5 to 6 cups sugar, depending on tartness of fruit
1/2 teaspoon salt
1/4 cup lemon juice
1/2 cup butter

Pastry:
1/2 recipe for regular pie pastry, or the cobbler crust recipe

THE PREPARATION

Drain the apricots, measure the juice and add water if necessary to make 1 1/2 quarts liquid. In 1/2 quart of the juice, add the cornstarch and stir until smooth. Bring the remainder of the juice to a boil and stir in the cornstarch paste. Cook and stir until the mixture is smooth and thick. Add the sugar and salt, and cook over low heat until the sugar is dissolved. Fold in the apricots gently, do not make a mush of them. Add the lemon juice and butter. Pour the mixture into one or two large baking pans, which have been buttered, and cover with the pastry. Brush the top of the pastry with melted butter, sprinkle with sugar, and bake at 400° for about 30 minutes or until brown.

CAKES AND COOKIES

PLAIN CAKE
a basic recipe

This recipe offers an untold number of opportunities for variations. It will make 50 servings, depending on the size of the pans used for the baking. If sliced lengthwise when baked in a sheet, filled with a custard sauce and frosted with a rich chocolate or lemon topping, it will make a delicious dessert.

To make 6 10-inch layers, or two large, oblong sheets

YOU WILL NEED
- 4 cups sugar
- 2 1/4 cups vegetable shortening or butter
- 10 eggs, separated
- 8 1/2 cups all-purpose flour
- 3 tablespoons baking powder
- 1 teaspoon salt
- 3 1/2 cups milk
- 2 teaspoons vanilla
- 2 teaspoons almond extract

THE PREPARATION

Cream the shortening and sugar until well blended and fluffy. Add the egg yolks and beat until well mixed. Sift the flour, salt, and baking powder twice, and add alternately with the milk to the first mixture. Beat just until the batter is smooth. Beat the egg whites until stiff and fold them into the batter. Add the flavorings. If baking in sheets, pour into a well-greased and floured baking pan, or pans, and bake at 350° for about 30 minutes or until the cake tests done. If baking in layers, pour into cake pans which are well greased and floured, and bake at 350° for about 25 minutes or until the layers test done.

WHITE CAKE

To make 1 pan 12 x 20 x 2 inches, sufficient cake to make 50 small servings

YOU WILL NEED
3 cups sugar
1 1/2 cups vegetable shortening
2 tablespoons baking powder
5 1/2 cups cake flour
1 teaspoon salt
8 egg whites
2 1/4 cups milk
1 tablespoon vanilla or 1 tablespoon almond flavoring

THE PREPARATION

Cream the sugar and shortening together and beat until the mixture is light and fluffy. Sift the flour with the salt and baking powder and add to the first mixture alternately with the milk. Stir or beat until well blended. Beat the egg whites until stiff and fold them into the batter carefully. Add flavoring and pour into a well-greased and floured baking pan. Bake at 350° for about 35 minutes or until the cake tests done. If the cake springs back when touched in the center with the fingers, it should be done.

SPONGE CAKE
an all-purpose

To make 50 servings, make this recipe twice

YOU WILL NEED
- 12 eggs, separated
- 2 cups sugar
- 2 cups all-purpose flour
- 2 teaspoons baking powder
- 2 tablespoons lemon juice
- 2 teaspoons lemon rind, grated
- 1/2 teaspoon salt
- 2 teaspoons vanilla

THE PREPARATION

Separate the eggs, and beat the yolks until light and slightly thick. Add 1 cup sugar to them with the lemon juice, rind, and vanilla. Sift the salt and baking powder with the flour and set aside. Beat the egg whites until stiff, but not dry, and while beating add the other cup of sugar little by little, beating well after each addition. Fold the yolk mixture alternately with the flour into the beaten whites. Fold carefully to keep the egg whites stiff. Grease a shallow baking pan or pans lightly on the bottom. Line with waxed paper and grease the paper lightly. Pour the mixture into the pan and spread it out evenly. The mixture should be smooth and rather thin. Bake in a preheated oven at 350° for 15 or 20 minutes, or until the cake springs back when touched lightly with the finger. Remove from oven and cool for a few minutes before taking the cake from the pan and removing the paper.

VARIATION

When the sheet is completely cold, split it through the center lengthwise to make 2 very thin layers. Fill with jelly or jam and frost the top with whipped cream. Then cut the cake into oblong shapes, squares, etc., for individual servings.

GERMAN'S SWEET CHOCOLATE CAKE

A cookbook of this type would be incomplete without this recipe. It is everybody's recipe.

To make one large cake of 16 to 18 servings

YOU WILL NEED

1 4-ounce package German's sweet chocolate
1/2 cup boiling water
4 eggs, separated
2 cups sugar
1 cup butter
2 1/2 cups all-purpose flour
3/4 cup buttermilk
1 teaspoon soda
2 teaspoons vanilla
1/2 teaspoon salt

The butter-pecan icing:
3 egg yolks
1 cup sugar
4 tablespoons butter
1 cup chopped pecan meats
1 cup undiluted evaporated milk
1 teaspoon vanilla

THE PREPARATION

Cream the shortening, sugar, and egg yolks, stir or beat until well blended. Dissolve the chocolate in the boiling water and add to the creamed mixture. Stir well. Sift the flour, salt, and soda together. Add the flour and buttermilk alternately to the first mixture. Beat or stir until smooth. Beat the egg whites until stiff and fold into the batter and add the vanilla. Bake in 2 10-inch greased and floured cake pans in a preheated oven at 350° for about 35 or 40 minutes or until the layers test done. Remove to cooling rack.

To make the icing: Mix all ingredients and stir until well blended. Cook over low heat, stirring constantly, until thick. Remove from heat and stir or beat again until cool and smooth. Add 1 cup of coconut for extra richness and to stretch the icing.

CHOCOLATE FUDGE CAKE

For something very special frost this cake with white chocolate icing. White chocolate can be found in many supermarkets, sold by the pound and not expensive. Or for a little more it can be obtained at the candy counter in department stores. This recipe makes 2 8-inch cakes (2 layers each) which will serve from 12 to 14 people. If the recipe is made twice that is sufficient for 50 generous servings.

To make 2 8-inch layer cakes

YOU WILL NEED

- 3 cups sugar
- 1 cup margarine
- 4 eggs
- 1/4 teaspoon salt
- 1 1/2 cups buttermilk
- 2 teaspoons soda
- 3 cups all-purpose flour
- 4 squares unsweetened chocolate
- 1 cup boiling water
- 2 teaspoons vanilla

THE PREPARATION

Dissolve the chocolate in 1 cup boiling water and set aside. Cream sugar and butter and beat in the eggs, one at a time, beating well after each addition. Stir in the chocolate and beat again until smooth. Sift the flour with soda and salt and add to the butter mixture alternately with the buttermilk. Do not overbeat. When mixture is blended, stir in the vanilla. The mixture will appear a little thin, but that is the nature of it. Pour into 4 8-inch well-greased and floured layer cake pans, and bake at 350° for about 35 minutes, or until the cake tests done. It should spring back when touched lightly in the center.

CARROT CAKE

To make approximately 25 servings

YOU WILL NEED
- 2 cups sugar
- 2 cups all-purpose flour
- 2 teaspoons soda
- 1 teaspoon salt
- 2 teaspoons cinnamon
- 1/2 teaspoon nutmeg
- 1 1/2 cups Wesson oil, or salad oil
- 4 eggs
- 3 cups grated carrots

Icing:
See cream cheese frosting recipe, p. 209

THE PREPARATION

Peel and grate the fresh carrots, or put them in a blender for 3 or 4 minutes, 1 cup at a time, and add to all other ingredients in a large mixing bowl. Beat the mixture until just blended. The batter will appear rather thin, but that is its nature; it bakes to a moist, firm cake. Pour into a well-greased and floured baking pan, approximately 18 x 10 x 2 inches, and bake at 350° for about 35 minutes or until the cake tests done. While the cake is still warm, spread it with cream cheese frosting, and cut in squares to serve.

RAW APPLE CAKE

My niece, Mary Bell Hoppel, of Laurel, Montana, who is not only a superb cook but also a consistent helper at cooking church suppers, has made this recipe for a long while. She shared it with me and I have enjoyed it and adapted it for quantity cooking. It is a rich, moist cake and actually gets better after being refrigerated for two or three days.

To make 25 servings, repeat this recipe once

YOU WILL NEED
- 2 eggs
- 4 cups raw, tart cooking apples, peeled and sliced thin
- 1/2 cup salad oil
- 2 cups sugar
- 1 teaspoon vanilla
- 1 teaspoon cinnamon
- 2 cups flour
- 2 teaspoons soda
- 1 1/2 cups finely chopped dates
- 1 cup pecans or English walnuts

THE PREPARATION

In a large mixing bowl break the eggs over the sliced raw apples, and stir until blended. Add all other ingredients and stir until well mixed. Pour into a 10 x 10-inch greased and floured baking pan and bake at 350° for 1 hour or until the cake is brown and done. For extra richness and to stretch the recipe add a dollop of sour cream to each serving.

DANISH SOUR CREAM COOKIES

To make 4 or 5 dozen, depending on size of the cookie

YOU WILL NEED
- 4 cups sugar
- 2 cups sweet cream butter
- 1/2 teaspoon salt
- 2 cups sour cream
- 4 eggs
- 2 teaspoons soda
- 5 cups all-purpose flour
- 2 teaspoons vanilla

THE PREPARATION

Cream the sugar with butter, add eggs, sour cream, salt, and vanilla. Beat or stir until well blended. Sift the soda with the flour and bind the entire mixture with sufficient flour to make a dough that will roll easily. It may take a little more flour than the 5 cups. Cut out to any desired size or shape and bake on a lightly greased baking sheet at 350° for about 20 minutes or until lightly brown.

PUDDINGS

ENGLISH TRIFLE DESSERT

The British make a delectable dessert something on the order of this recipe, and add fruit and a flavored gelatin. When they are asked "what do you put in it," they say, "a trifle of this and a trifle of that." Perhaps that is where the name originated.

To make approximately 50 servings

YOU WILL NEED
- 4 commercial angel food cakes, about 1 pound each
- 4 quarts milk, hot
- 2 cups sugar
- 2 dozen eggs
- 1 quart heavy cream, whipped
- 4 tablespoons grated orange rind

THE PREPARATION

Prepare the cake ahead by slicing each crosswise into two parts. Then cut each half into ten pieces. Lay the pieces on the bottom of baking pans or in casseroles which are approximately 2 inches or more in depth. Set aside. Beat the eggs with the sugar until light and slightly thick. Heat the milk to the boiling point, but do not boil. While the milk is still hot, pour it very slowly into the beaten eggs, beating the mixture as it is being combined. Return the whole mixture to the kettle and with a wooden spoon stir constantly while the custard cooks slowly over low heat. When the custard becomes slightly thick and coats the back of the spoon, remove from the heat. If it should curdle, and it often does, beat it again until entirely smooth. Set aside to cool. When cool, stir in the orange rind and fold in the whipped cream. Pour the custard over the cake pieces slowly, allowing the custard to be absorbed somewhat by the cake. Refrigerate several hours before serving. Serve with a spoonful of whipped cream on the top of each serving, and with grated orange rind on top of the cream, for an attractive garnish.

SWEET ROLL PUDDING

This pudding is a bit richer than the old bread pudding, but not any more expensive. It can be served with a dessert sauce or whipped cream or just as it is. To serve it hot, whether freshly made or reheated, makes a very special dessert for any meal.

To make approximately 50 servings

YOU WILL NEED
- 3 dozen cinnamon rolls, commercial or homemade (average size)
- 4 quarts milk, hot
- 12 eggs, beaten
- 1 teaspoon salt
- 1 1/2 cups sugar
- 1/2 cup butter
- 1/2 cup flour
- 1 cup raisins
- 1 tablespoon grated orange rind
- 1 teaspoon nutmeg

THE PREPARATION

Break the cinnamon rolls into small pieces and spread evenly over the bottom of a large baking pan, or pans. Heat the butter and stir in the flour, stirring and cooking for 2 or 3 minutes, or until blended. Gradually add the milk, stirring and cooking slowly until the mixture is well blended and slightly thick. Beat the eggs until creamy and a little thick, add the sugar and salt and blend. Combine the two mixtures, adding the eggs to the milk gradually. Stir until smooth. Fold in the raisins, nutmeg, and orange rind, and mix well. Taste for sweetness and add a little more sugar if needed. Pour the custard slowly over the rolls, and bake at 350° for about 40 minutes or until the pudding is brown and well set.

PRUNE WHIP MOLD

To make approximately 50 servings

YOU WILL NEED
- 5 1-tablespoon packages unflavored gelatin
- 2 cups cold water
- 2 quarts prune purée, sieved
- 2 1/2 cups prune juice, hot
- 1 1/2 cups sugar
- 1 cup orange juice
- 1 tablespoon orange rind, grated
- 8 egg whites, beaten with 1 cup sugar
- 1 pint heavy cream, whipped
- 1 cup almonds, toasted and ground

THE PREPARATION

Sprinkle the gelatin over the cold water. Bring the prune juice to a boil and add the softened gelatin. Stir until completely dissolved. Set aside to cool. When cool, add the orange juice, rind, and sugar and stir until smooth. Fold in the prune purée and set over ice, or refrigerate until the mixture begins to thicken. Whip the egg white until stiff, fold in the 1 cup sugar, and as soon as the prune mixture has reached a slightly thickened stage, fold in the egg whites. Refrigerate again for a short time, watching that the gelatin does not become too thick. Whip the cream and fold a portion of it into the gelatin mixture, reserve some of it to spread over the top of mold. Spoon or pour the gelatin into the mold. Refrigerate for several hours before serving. Unmold and spread with remaining whipped cream before serving, and sprinkle the almonds over the cream. A delightful and unusual dessert.

LIME MOLD with Angel Food Cake

My good friend and neighbor, Julie Remley, gave us a sample of this dessert once and we liked it so much that I asked for the recipe. I have made it many times since, and have now adapted it for quantity cooking.

To make approximately 25 servings, 2 loaf-pan molds

YOU WILL NEED

4 3-ounce packages lime gelatin
6 cups boiling water
2 cups juice from canned pears
4 cups canned pears, sliced
1 cup flaky coconut
1 cup sugar
1 angel food cake, cubed (about 1 pound size)
1 pint heavy cream, whipped
shredded unsweetened chocolate for top

THE PREPARATION

Dissolve the gelatin in the boiling water and stir until blended. To hasten the cooling, set the bowl over a pan of ice or ice water. Prepare two loaf pans, about 9 1/2 x 5 1/2 x 2 1/2-inches each, by rinsing in cold water. Have all ingredients assembled and ready to add as the gelatin begins to thicken. Add the sugar and coconut to the gelatin as it cools. When the gelatin begins to thicken a little, pour enough in the mold to cover the bottom about 1/2 inch in depth. Refrigerate to hasten the congealing. When this bottom portion has set, start adding the other ingredients. First, spread a layer of sliced pears, then a layer of whipped cream, slightly sweetened, then a layer of cubed angel food cake. Spoon the thickened gelatin over this, allowing the gelatin to dribble onto the cake pieces. Continue building the molds until all ingredients are used, but make the gelatin come out on top. Reserve some of the whipped cream for spreading on the mold when it has been unmolded. Refrigerate for several hours or overnight. A few hours before the serving, unmold and spread the tops with the whipped cream and sprinkle shredded, unsweetened chocolate over the cream. To serve, slice with a very sharp knife to keep the colors and ingredients in order.

FROSTINGS, ICINGS,

Baker's frosting. Add 1 or 2 teaspoons hot water and 1/2 teaspoon vanilla to 1 cup powdered sugar and stir to make a thin paste. Use this mixture to spread over hot sweet breads, hot rolls with fruits and nuts in them, cookies, doughnuts, muffins, and so on, as they come from the oven.

Cream-cheese frosting. Combine 1 stick unsalted margarine, 1 8-ounce package cream cheese, 4 or 5 cups powdered sugar, 1/2 cup pecans, and 1 teaspoon vanilla together and beat until thick enough to spread and stay set. Add the sugar a little at a time and use only the amount needed.

Mocha butter cream. In an electric mixer beat 1/2 pound sweet cream butter until fluffy, then beat in 3/4 cup sugar, 2 teaspoons instant coffee crystals, and 1 tablespoon dark cocoa dissolved in 1 tablespoon hot water, and beat until well blended. Use for frosting and decorating elaborate desserts or pastry specialties.

Cocoa frosting. To 1/3 cup hot strong coffee, add 4 tablespoons sweet cream butter, 1/2 cup cocoa, and a sprinkle of salt. Stir until well mixed and cocoa is dissolved. Add about 4 cups of powdered sugar, or sufficient to make a spreading mixture. Add vanilla and 1/2 cup chopped pecans, if desired.

WHITE CHOCOLATE FROSTING

This chocolate can be found in many supermarkets or in the candy section of department stores. It is less expensive in supermarkets, but worth the price no matter where it is found. This recipe makes an excellent frosting for chocolate cakes or for a spread on party cookies.

To make frosting to cover 1 8-inch two-layer cake

YOU WILL NEED
- 4-ounces white chocolate or 1/2 cup grated and packed into cup
- 3 tablespoons milk
- 1/2 cup butter or margarine, softened
- 3 to 4 cups powdered sugar
- 1 teaspoon vanilla

THE PREPARATION

In a small saucepan placed over hot water, heat the grated chocolate with the milk until dissolved. Stir until smooth and keep warm. In a large mixing bowl, beat the butter until fluffy, add other ingredients and beat until thick and smooth. Add more sugar if necessary to make a spreading mixture that will stay set.

CHOCOLATE FUDGE FROSTING

To make sufficient frosting for 2 3-layer cakes, or two large sheet cakes

YOU WILL NEED
- 2 1/2 cups brown sugar
- 2 1/2 cups white sugar
- 6 ounces unsweetened chocolate
- 1 13-ounce can evaporated milk, plus 1/4 cup water
- sprinkle of salt
- 1/2 teaspoon cream of tartar
- 4 tablespoons butter
- 2 teaspoons vanilla

THE PREPARATION

Mix the sugars, salt, cream of tartar and milk. Melt the chocolate over hot water and add to the first mixture. In a heavy saucepan, cook the mixture until it forms a soft ball when dropped into cold water. Stir often as it cooks to prevent burning. Remove from heat and add vanilla and butter. Stir or beat until cool. If it is too thick, thin with cream or evaporated milk until it is thin enough to spread.

> Spice a dish with love, and it pleases every palate.
> (A Latin Proverb)

FILLINGS AND SWEET SAUCES

Pastry Cream Filling. Scald 1 1/2 cups milk. Mix 1/2 cup sugar with 4 egg yolks and beat until creamy. Add 1/4 cup flour and continue beating until blended. Gradually add this mixture to the scalded milk, stirring and beating until all of it is included. Pour back into the saucepan and cook, stirring vigorously until it reaches the boiling point, but do not boil. Remove from heat, add 1 teaspoon vanilla and 1/2 teaspoon almond flavoring, strain, and cool. Excellent for a spread between cake layers.

To make chocolate cream filling. Add 2 squares unsweetened chocolate when scalding the milk, and add sugar to taste, to the pastry cream filling above.

To make mocha cream filling. Add 1/4 cup instant coffee crystals to the milk when it is scalding. Cover for 15 minutes and let stand. Strain and proceed as for pastry cream.

CREAM FILLING

Use this filling for Boston cream pies, between layers of other cakes, or as a dessert. There are countless ways to serve this rich and creamy filling, and many variations that can be made with it.

To make sufficient filling for 4 2-layer cakes

YOU WILL NEED	4 1/2 cups milk, with 1 13-ounce can undiluted evaporated milk as a part of the milk 2/3 cup flour 3 tablespoons cornstarch 1 cup sugar 4 egg yolks 4 tablespoons butter or margarine 1/2 teaspoon salt 2 teaspoons vanilla 1 cup heavy cream, whipped (optional)

THE PREPARATION

Heat the milk over hot water. Blend the flour, cornstarch, and 1/2 cup sugar. Add 1 cup, or a little more, of the hot milk to this mixture and stir until it forms a smooth paste. Add this mixture to the remainder of the milk and cook over low heat, stirring until smooth and thick. Beat the egg yolks and combine with the other 1/2 cup sugar. Gradually add to the hot milk, stirring constantly. Cook about 5 minutes over low heat. Remove the mixture from the heat, add butter, salt, and vanilla and cool. If using the cream, beat it until it holds a stiff peak and fold gently into the custard when the custard is cool.

LEMON FILLING or Sauce

To make filling for 3 2-layer cakes

YOU WILL NEED	2 cups sugar 3 cups water 7 tablespoons cornstarch, blended into 3/4 cup cold water 4 egg yolks 1 tablespoon grated lemon rind 1/3 cup lemon juice 2 tablespoons butter 1/2 cup heavy cream, whipped

THE PREPARATION

Heat the water and sugar together. Blend the cornstarch with the cold water and add to the hot water and sugar. Cook slowly, stirring until thickened and clear. Beat the egg yolks until lemon colored and add a portion of the hot mixture very slowly to the beaten yolks. Beat until blended. Return to the remainder of hot mixture and cook for about 5 minutes more. Stir to prevent lumping and sticking. Remove from heat, add lemon rind, juice, and butter. Cool. Whip the cream until it holds a stiff peak and fold into the custard.

VANILLA CUSTARD
a basic recipe

This is a custard, or sweet sauce, that answers many purposes. It can be used for filling cream puffs; as a filling for layer cakes; as part of a fruit dessert; over puddings; or topped with a bit of whipped cream and served as a custard dessert.

To make approximately 2 1/2 quarts

YOU WILL NEED
- 2 quarts milk, hot
- 10 egg yolks
- 1 cup sugar
- 6 tablespoons cornstarch
- 1/4 teaspoon salt
- 1 tablespoon vanilla
- 1 cup heavy cream whipped (optional)

THE PREPARATION

Heat the milk to hot, but do not boil. Stir the sugar, salt, and cornstarch together until well blended. Add the egg yolks and beat until the mixture is thick and lemon colored. While beating the eggs, add the hot milk gradually. Return to the heat and cook slowly, stirring constantly, until the mixture is thick. If it should curdle, remove from heat and beat vigorously, either by hand or with electric mixer. Add vanilla. The custard should be thick enough to hold its shape. If desired, add the whipped cream at this point. Chill.

VARIATION

Coconut custard—2 1/2 quarts
2 quarts vanilla custard
1 cup moist flakey coconut
1 cup heavy cream, whipped

Combine, chill, and serve as needed.

VARIATION II

Orange custard 2 1/2 quarts
2 quarts vanilla custard
1/2 cup strained orange juice
1 tablespoon grated orange rind

Combine and chill. Serve over fruits, or spread between layer cakes.

CHOCOLATE CUSTARD

To make 2 1/2 quarts

YOU WILL NEED

2 quarts milk, hot
1 cup sugar
8 egg yolks
6 ounces chocolate, melted (unsweetened)
6 tablespoons cornstarch
1 tablespoon vanilla

THE PREPARATION

Combine the sugar and cornstarch, stir until blended. Add the egg yolks and with electric beater beat the mixture until the eggs are thick and lemon colored. Bring the milk to a boil, but do not boil. Over hot water, melt the chocolate. Combine with hot milk and gradually add to the eggs, beating constantly. Return the mixture to the kettle and cook over low heat, stirring constantly until the mixture thickens. If it separates, beat again until it is smooth. Stir in the vanilla and cool.

STRAWBERRY CREAM CHEESE SAUCE

To make approximately 1 1/2 quarts

YOU WILL NEED
- 2 8-ounce packages cream cheese, softened
- 4 cups sliced fresh strawberries, or an equal amount of some other fruit
- 1/2 cup sugar
- 1/3 cup lemon juice
- 2 cups heavy cream, whipped

THE PREPARATION

Soften the cheese and combine with the sugar and lemon juice. Stir until blended. Fold in the fruit, but do not beat; keep the fruit intact, if possible. Fold in the whipped cream and taste for sweetening. Add more sugar if needed.

VARIATION

Omit the strawberries and add 1 cup finely chopped dates and 1 cup well-drained crushed pineapple.

Surely there is something akin to the Divine
In preparing for and feeding mankind.
—S. Morgan

PART IV

CASSEROLES

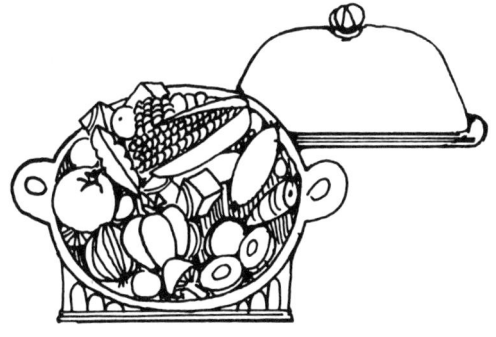

CASSEROLES

For years, casserole referred to the container, or dish, made of a coarse clay and of such quality as to be oven proof. It could be placed on the table as it came from the oven with its cooked food and double as an attractive serving bowl.

The casserole as we know it today has gone through several periods of development. There was a time when the man of the house turned up his nose at the thought of a casserole for dinner. He thought of it as a mass of leftovers, concocted with a sauce of some kind, baked and named "super" or "supreme" to disguise its origin.

Now the casserole has come into its own. It is no longer only a container that functions in two or three capacities, but one whose contents are put together with a degree of skill in matching or combining ingredients to increase nutrition, flavor, and with appeal to the appetite.

There are a number of advantages to the *casserole syndrome* for church suppers. One of the best things is that the casserole, almost without exception, can be made days ahead, frozen, and baked when needed in the same dish or baking pan that it has been frozen in. This helps to make the cook's work schedule flexible and at the same time assures her of a delicious meal prepared in short order.

The basic casseroles are a combination of meats and vegetables *and sauces* that do the blending. With appropriate seasonings added to enhance the flavor and garnish to add appetite appeal, the casserole is something to look forward to. A special thanks for the day of the casserole—especially for church suppers.

BROCCOLI AND RICE

To make approximately 50 servings

YOU WILL NEED

2 1/2 pounds rice
salt, if needed
6 pounds frozen broccoli, chopped
6 10 1/2-ounce cans cream of chicken soup
1 cup celery, thinly sliced
1/2 cup onions, minced
3/4 cup margarine
1/2 cup mayonnaise
3 to 4 cups cracker crumbs
1 teaspoon white pepper (optional)

THE PREPARATION

Prepare the rice according to package directions, or see recipe p. 183. Cook the broccoli according to package directions, or drop the frozen broccoli into a small amount of salted water and cook just until tender, about 20 minutes. Heat the margarine and sauté the celery and onions until both are tender. Add the mayonnaise and pepper, and stir until blended. In a large mixing bowl, combine all ingredients, except the cracker crumbs. Stir until thoroughly blended. Pour the mixture into greased baking pans, or in oven-proof casserole bowls, sprinkle generously with the cracker crumbs and bake at 350° for about 30 minutes, or until the mixture is slightly brown. The dish should be well set but it does not hold its shape when spooned out. Serve hot.

BEEF CUBES AND CABBAGE

To make approximately 50 servings

YOU WILL NEED
- 6 pounds, crisp, fresh cabbage, coarsely shredded
- 5 pounds lean beef, cubed
- salt
- pepper
- 1/2 cup margarine or butter
- 2 1/2 quarts white sauce
- 3 to 4 cups bread crumbs, made with whole wheat bread

THE PREPARATION

Prepare the cabbage by cooking in salted boiling water, uncovered, for about 6 or 7 minutes. It should be almost tender. It will finish cooking in the oven. Heat the butter and sauté the beef cubes until the pink disappears. While the beef is cooking, sprinkle sparingly with salt and pepper. The cabbage will have been salted, and the white sauce will have salt; therefore, salt with caution. Lift the cabbage from the salty water, and in a large mixing bowl combine it with all other ingredients except the bread crumbs. Pour the mixture into one or two large casseroles and sprinkle with the bread crumbs. Bake for about 25 minutes or until slightly brown. The mixture should be very moist, but not soupy. Grated sharp cheese may be added with the bread crumbs or instead of bread crumbs.

Enough is as good as a feast.

CHICKEN AND TORTILLAS
with Green Chilis

If you like a touch of Old Mexico in some of your cooking, this casserole will please you. If you are not accustomed to using green chiles for a bold seasoning, just this once, be brave.

To make approximately 50 servings

YOU WILL NEED
- 5 to 6 pounds chicken, cooked, boned, and cubed (about 18 pounds before cooking)
- 1 quart chicken broth
- 1/2 cup flour
- 1/2 cup margarine
- 1 cup onions, chopped
- 1 1/2 quarts canned tomatoes, chopped
- 6 cups milk
- 2 4-ounce canned green chilis, seeded and sliced
- salt
- 4 dozen tortillas, canned, frozen, or fresh, pulled into pieces
- 2 pounds grated sharp cheese

THE PREPARATION

Melt the margarine, add the onions and sauté for about 5 minutes. Add the flour and cook until bubbly. Pour in the milk and broth gradually and stir until thick and smooth. Add the chilis and tomatoes to the sauce and stir well. Salt if needed. In two large greased baking pans, spread a layer of the chicken, a layer of tortillas, and a layer of the grated cheese. Pour sauce over this and continue the process until all ingredients are used. Bake at 375° until slightly brown and blended. Serve very hot.

CHICKEN WITH YELLOW SQUASH

To make approximately 50 servings

YOU WILL NEED
- 5 pounds cooked chicken breasts, boned and cubed
- 8 pounds yellow squash, young and tender
- 2 teaspoons white pepper
- salt
- 2 1/2 quarts white sauce
- 1/2 cup mayonnaise
- 3 1/2 cups bread crumbs, made from whole wheat bread

THE PREPARATION

Prepare the chicken ahead and reserve the stock in which it is cooked. Prepare the squash by scrubbing it well, trimming all blemishes, and cutting away the ends. Cut the squash away from the seeds and discard them. Drop the squash pieces into the reserved chicken stock and cook until barely tender, about 10 minutes. Remove from stock and set aside. Make the white sauce, using at least 1 quart of the stock. Stir in the mayonnaise and pepper. Add salt, if needed. Taste for seasonings and correct as necessary. Combine the chicken and squash and pour into buttered baking pans, or into large oven-proof dishes. Cover with the white sauce, then with the bread crumbs. Bake at 375° for about 30 minutes or until the casserole is slightly brown and is blended and set. It should be very moist, but not soupy.

CORN AND TOMATO CASSEROLE

To make approximately 50 servings

YOU WILL NEED
- 1 No. 10 can whole kernel corn
- 4 quarts canned tomatoes, the peeled variety, chopped & drained
- 1 cup chopped onions
- 1 cup butter or bacon fat
- 1 cup green peppers, cut in strips
- 1/3 cup sugar
- 2 tablespoons salt
- 1/2 teaspoon black pepper
- 4 cups grated cheese
- 4 cups potato chips, crumbled

THE PREPARATION

Heat the fat and sauté the onions and green peppers until tender. Add the pepper and the drained tomatoes and cook slowly for about 15 minutes, or until the mixture is well blended. Combine with the corn and add the salt slowly. Stir in the sugar. Taste for seasonings. Pour the mixture into two greased baking pans and sprinkle first with the cheese and then with the potato chip crumbs. Bake at 375° for about 30 minutes, or until slightly brown and well blended. If too much liquid accumulates for easy serving, spoon it off. This is an excellent hot dish to serve with cold cuts and garlic-buttered hot French bread.

CRAB AND SHRIMP CASSEROLE

To make approximately 50 servings

YOU WILL NEED
- 5 pounds crabmeat
- 5 pounds shrimp, cooked, peeled, and deveined
- 2 1/2 quarts canned tomatoes, drained
- 1 cup finely chopped onions
- 1 cup green peppers, thinly sliced
- 1 cup thinly sliced celery
- 1/2 cup salad oil
- 1 bay leaf
- 2 garlic cloves, minced
- 1/4 teaspoon cayenne pepper
- 2 pounds rice
- salt

THE PREPARATION

In a large saucepan heat the oil and sauté onions, celery, and peppers until they are tender. Add all the seasonings and the drained tomatoes and cook gently for about 15 minutes or until blended. Salt according to need, about 2 teaspoons. After the mixture is well blended, remove the bay leaf. Cook the rice according to package directions (or see recipe p. 183), and keep hot until other ingredients are ready. In a large kettle, combine all ingredients, add crab and shrimp gently to keep the pieces intact. Place over heat and cook slowly for about 15 minutes. The shellfish cooks quickly, almost by the time it is thoroughly hot. Serve in individual bowls for best results, and with a slice of French bread which is hot and buttered.

HAM AND RED BEANS with Fritos

This combination is a favorite in the Southwest. It makes a very satisfying meal with only a drink and a light dessert.

To make approximately 50 servings

YOU WILL NEED
- 4 pounds ham, cooked and diced
- 4 quarts red beans, cooked, seasoned, and well drained
- 2 garlic cloves, minced
- 1/2 cup brown sugar
- 1/2 cup vinegar
- 4 tablespoons horseradish
- 4 tablespoons prepared mustard
- 1 1/2 cups catsup
- 2 quarts Fritos, crumbled

THE PREPARATION

Mix all ingredients, except the Fritos, and stir until well blended. Pour the mixture into well-greased baking pans, sprinkle generously with the crumbled Fritos. Bake at 375° for about 30 minutes, or until slightly brown and well blended. For a richer casserole add grated sharp cheese on top of Fritos before baking.

TUNA AND NOODLE CASSEROLE

To make approximately 50 servings

YOU WILL NEED
- 5 pounds tuna, flaked (water packed preferred)
- 2 1/2 pounds noodles
- salt, if needed
- 2 1/2 quarts white sauce
- 1 teaspoon black pepper
- 1/2 cup mayonnaise
- 1 cup pimientos, minced
- 1 pound sharp cheese, grated
- 2 cups bread crumbs, use day-old French bread

THE PREPARATION

Prepare the noodles according to package directions, and keep hot. Salt sparingly in this recipe. The sauce will be salted, the noodles will have salt, and the tuna is very salty by nature. Make the white sauce, add the mayonnaise, pimientos, and pepper. Combine the tuna and noodles with the white sauce and pour into two large baking pans. Sprinkle first with the cheese and then with the French bread crumbs. The French bread crumbs give this casserole a most unusual and satisfying flavor.

SPINACH AND TURKEY CASSEROLE

My good friend, Sally Wilder from Fort Worth, Texas, who is not only a connoisseur of excellent foods, but of art and decor as well, gave me this recipe. I have altered it somewhat from the original to make it more practical for quantity cookery, but in substance it is the same recipe. The recipe is rather detailed and time-consuming but a real gourmet dish at the finish.

To make 25 generous servings

YOU WILL NEED
- 2 5-6 pound uncooked turkey breasts, or 1 12-pound uncooked turkey breast
- water to cover
- 2 tablespoons salt
- 4 tablespoons peppercorns
- 3 cups carrots, peeled and sliced
- 1 cup celery, sliced
- 3 to 4 pounds fresh spinach
- 1/2 cup butter
- 2 quarts turkey stock
- 1 pound tiny noodles
- 3/4 cup flour
- 1/4 teaspoon nutmeg
- 1/2 teaspoon oregano
- 2 cups light cream
- 2 cups grated sharp cheese

THE PREPARATION

Cook the turkey breasts in a large kettle, with water to cover, add salt, peppercorns, celery, and carrots. Bring to a boil, then reduce heat and simmer for about 4 hours, or until the bird is quite tender. Reserve the stock. Cool and remove bones and skin. Cut into small pieces. Rinse the spinach and cook it briefly, about 8 to 10 minutes, in about 1 1/2 cups water. Drain well and toss it lightly with 2 tablespoons melted butter. Sprinkle it with salt, pepper, and the nutmeg. Melt the butter in a large saucepan, stir in the flour, and cook until blended. Gradually add turkey stock and cook for about 30 minutes, stirring occasionally. Add the cream and oregano and cook about 5 minutes longer.

Cook the noodles according to package directions, or just until tender; do not overcook, they will be reheated in the sauce. Drain them. In one or two large casseroles, or baking pans, make layers of noodles, spinach, then turkey and continue the layers until all ingredients are used. Pour the sauce over the layers and sprinkle generously with the cheese. Bake in a preheated oven at 375° until the mixture is heated through and slightly brown. The casserole can be placed under the broiler to brown, if desired, after some baking.

PART V

A SHORT CULINARY TRAVELOGUE

EATING WITH SOME OTHER COUNTRIES

This section is a short culinary travelogue which, I hope, brings to the church supper highlights of a few European and Mexican kitchens. For each country represented here, I have included a bit of food history, giving some of the most popular dishes, with a menu and a few recipes to complete the menu.

I have visited many of these countries, enjoyed their foods, and collected their recipes.

It is my sincere hope that this section will enhance the worldwide vision of the church.

DENMARK

Denmark, being a cluster of little islands, can obviously be expected to have fish as one of its main foods. It has many and varied types of fish dishes, and many dishes of fish combined with other meats. The Danish make great use of shellfish. Their shrimp for the most part is of a tiny variety, a special species. In fact, their open sandwiches, which are world famous, might include two or three varieties of fish on a single sandwich.

Most of their breads are rye and dark breads. The rye bread forms the foundation for the open sandwich, which is served with heaped-up foods in tasty and hearty combinations.

Danish pastry is light and flaky beyond belief, and what is served under the name of Danish pastry in many other countries is generally a very poor imitation of the real thing. They also serve delicious coffee breads, rich puddings, and cakes.

A Church Supper Featuring Danish Foods

Open Sandwiches   Relish Plates
Platter of Cheeses   Danish Apple Cake
Coffee with Heavy Cream

OPEN SANDWICHES

To make these use a large slice of dark rye bread cut lengthwise of the loaf, spread with sweet cream butter and add one of the following combinations:

1. 1 dozen tiny shrimp, cooked and deveined; 1 slice of thin pork, rolled around 1 long, thin marinated cucumber; 2 pickled herring; shredded lettuce; 1 deviled egg; 2 slices raw onion; 1 slice thin roast beef.

2. 6 oysters, marinated in wine sauce; 2 smoked herring; dried beef wrapped around onion slices; roast potatoes, cubed; cooked cabbage wedge; lettuce wedge; and olives. All of these are placed in attractive arrangement on the slice of bread.

DANISH APPLE CAKE

To make approximately 25 servings or 2 large loaves

YOU WILL NEED
- 6 cups bread crumbs
- 3/4 cup butter
- 2 quarts sweetened applesauce
- 1 tablespoon grated orange rind
- 4 teaspoons cinnamon
- 2 cups chopped nuts
- 1 pint heavy cream, whipped and slightly sweetened
- candied apple rings for garnish (optional)

THE PREPARATION

Heat the butter and sauté the bread crumbs until they are slightly brown. Mix the applesauce, orange rind, cinnamon, and nuts together. In 2 large well-buttered loaf pans, spread first a layer of bread crumbs, then a layer of applesauce mixture, and so on until all ingredients are used. The top layer should be bread crumbs. Dot this with butter and bake at 350° for about 30 minutes. Remove from oven and when cool, spread the tops with the whipped cream. This is a rich, tasty dessert which can be frozen and reheated later when needed.

FRANCE

The French look upon gastronomy as a fine art, ranking with literature, music, and some of the sciences. It is said that the French have conquered the world of foods with their *haute cuisine* and *cuisine classique*. However, the chief rules of their cuisine are actually very simple. Centuries ago they said "nature is the best cook." If you choose high-grade ingredients, handle with care and patience, you will bring out the true and natural flavors, which is superb cooking. Cooking as an advanced art was actually introduced into France during the Renaissance when Italian princesses married into French royalty and brought with them from Italy their cooks and their food knowledge.

We find today on our menus French terms, very familiar to most people who eat at good restaurants. They are so familiar to us that we seldom remember anything about their origin. Among the numerous terms are entrée, sauce, salad, dessert, soufflé, omelet, purée, casserole, chiffon, meringue, and many others.

The food of France consists of an endless variety. Fish is in abundance; meats and vegetables with wine sauces, mushrooms, soups, exquisite salads, served mostly with an oil-and-vinegar dressing, and desserts are unequaled anywhere. For desserts some of their specialties are crêmes, charlottes, fruit soufflés, parfaits, sherbets, and exquisitely prepared pâtisseries.

A Church Supper Featuring French Foods

	French Onion Soup	
Pot Roast		Baked Tomatoes
	Lettuce Salad	
French Bread		Lemon Custard in Pastry Shells
	Wine	
	Café au Lait	

The recipes required for all the dishes listed on this menu can be found in PART III of this book.

GERMANY

The Germans have always been considered hard workers and heavy eaters. Their food is largely of the filling kind, consisting mostly of thick soups, potatoes, dark breads, sausages, meats, and vegetables. There are, also, meat-and-vegetable-combination casseroles, cheeses, and always rich, wonderful desserts. They often place a helping of whipped cream on the richest of desserts as a finish to a full and hearty meal. But they take their work and exercises seriously and they continue to be a nation of hearty and healthy people.

They make much of sweet and sour meats, pickled and marinated meats, and fish of all types and kinds. They serve beer with most of their heavy meals and cheese dishes, and wine with nearly all full meals.

Their desserts, found in the exquisite *Konditoreien* are unsurpassed and offer a rich variety of fancy cakes, torten, and decorated and appetizing other desserts.

If you want to indulge yourself, stop by one of these shops the next time you are in Germany and have a real *kaffeeklatsch*.

A Church Supper Featuring German Foods

Sweet and Sour Wieners   Hot Potato Salad
Creamed Cabbage   Relishes and Cheeses
Wine
Pumpernickel Bread   German Streusel Cake
Coffee

The recipe for German streusel cake is given here and the recipes for all other dishes on the menu are found in PART III of this book.

GERMAN STREUSEL CAKE

To make a streusel cake that cuts from 14 to 16 slices

YOU WILL NEED
1 package active dry yeast
1/3 cup lukewarm water
4 tablespoons soft butter
2 tablespoons sugar
1/2 teaspoon salt
2 eggs
1 tablespoon grated lemon rind
1/2 cup lukewarm milk
2 to 3 cups all-purpose flour

Streusel topping:
1/4 cup butter
1/2 cup sugar
1 cup flour
1 teaspoon cinnamon

THE PREPARATION

Dissolve the yeast in lukewarm water and set aside. Cream the butter, sugar, and salt. Stir in the eggs, lemon rind, and then add the yeast, milk, and about one-half of the flour. Stir or beat until smooth. Gradually add the remainder of the flour, mixing and kneading until the dough is firm but still soft. Place in a well-greased, deep bowl, cover, and set aside to double in bulk. When doubled, punch it down, turn it over, and once more cover and let rise until doubled in bulk. While the dough is rising the second time, prepare the streusel topping by mixing all ingredients together, cutting them with a fork until crumbly.

Pat or roll out the dough on a lightly floured surface, place in a greased, round baking pan, brush with melted butter, then sprinkle generously with the streusel mixture. Press down lightly. Let rise about 20 minutes, then bake in hot oven at 400° for about 30 minutes or until brown and the cake tests done.

HUNGARY

Before the twin cities of Buda and Pest became one, they formed a gay and colorful center to which tourists flocked. People visited there not only for their historical monuments and architectural masterpieces, but also for the gypsy music, the excellent wines, and most of all the good foods.

Although their foods resemble a combination of many of the European countries, their seasonings are somewhat different. The most distinctive characteristic is the use of red pimiento and paprika. Most of their meat, fish, and vegetable dishes have an exotic look to them and a high color of red from the use of paprika and pimiento. They even make a cheese which is colored and flavored with paprika. Horseradish, dill, and caraway seed are also used often.

Hungarian goulash is internationally unchallenged as the most widely accepted dish. It had its beginning with the wandering herdsmen who invented it to use what they called shepherd's meats. Stuffed cabbage roll is another Hungarian specialty. Hungarian meals usually end with plates of cheeses and fresh fruits or with rich and filling desserts.

A Church Supper Featuring Hungarian Foods

Stuffed Cabbage Roll   Steamed Rice with Piminto
              Relish Plates
Dark Rye Bread with   Fresh Fruits with Cheeses
Sweet Cream Butter
                    Wine
                    Coffee

The recipe for stuffed cabbage roll is given here and the recipes required for all other dishes on the menu can be found in PART III of this book.

HUNGARIAN CABBAGE ROLL

To make 25 servings

YOU WILL NEED

2 large cabbage heads with loose crisp, leaves
boiling water
4 pounds coarsely ground beef
1 pound pork sausage, seasoned
4 eggs
1/2 cup uncooked rice
2 tablespoons Worcestershire sauce
2 teaspoons salt

The sauce:
2 quarts peeled canned tomatoes
1 cup finely chopped onions
1/2 cup sliced pimiento
1 tablespoon paprika
1/2 cup butter
4 slices chopped bacon
1/8 teaspoon cayenne pepper
1 teaspoon thyme
2 tablespoons sesame seeds
1/2 teaspoon nutmeg
2 bay leaves

THE PREPARATION

Prepare the sauce first by melting the butter in a large roasting pan on top of the stove. Sauté the onion and the bacon pieces in the fat. Add tomatoes and seasonings, and simmer slowly for about 30 minutes.

Remove bruised outer leaves from cabbage heads and cut around the stalk to loosen top of leaves. Drop the cabbage into a kettle of boiling water and remove from fire at once. Let stand for 5 or 6 minutes or until the leaves pull away from the head easily and are soft enough to roll without breaking. Remove at least 25 large leaves from the head, drain, and set aside.

Season the beef with salt and Worcestershire sauce. Add the eggs and uncooked rice, and blend. Add sausage and mix well. Divide the meat into the same number of parts as cabbage leaves and place it on the center of the leaf. Roll and tuck the leaves in such a manner as to prevent the mixture from spilling out. Arrange the rolls carefully in the warm sauce mixture. If stacked, the sauce should be deep enough to keep the top rolls covered. Cover the roaster with a lid and bake at 375° for about 1 1/2 hours or until the rolls are completely tender and blended with the sauce. These can be served over hot rice with some of the sauce spooned over each helping. Garnish with sprigs of parsley.

ITALY

Italian food tells much of that nation's history which had its beginning in turmoil. In fact, Italy was not unified as a single country until the late 19th century. There were, of course, many and various regional and local habits of food preparation and serving. The names of many of their foods and especially of their wines still carry the names of local or provincial sections of the country.

Italy's pasta is one of the main dishes and has many and varied concepts. All of the pastas such as spaghetti, macaroni, noodles, and gnocchi, are prepared and cooked in a multitude of different ways and often served in beautiful style.

Seasonings of herbs and spices have always played a significant part in Italian food preparation. Thyme, bay leaf, basil, dill, oregano, and many others have added tantalizing aromas to their menus. Some sections of Italy use garlic, but not all parts of the country. Cheeses are a very important part of the diet.

Their flair for desserts is known all over the world. You may find a dessert of fresh fruit and cheese on the table, depending on how much pasta was served. Or, their expertise in ice-cream making may bring on a dessert of ice cream, topped with whipped cream, shredded candied fruits, and nuts.

A Church Supper Featuring Italian Foods

Lasagne Old Style   Vegetable Salad
                    Wine
French Bread   Spumoni
                    Coffee

The recipe for Spumoni is given here and the recipes required for other parts of the menu can be found in PART III of this book.

SPUMONI

To make approximately 25 servings

YOU WILL NEED
- 3 quarts vanilla ice cream
- 1 quart heavy cream, whipped, slightly sweetened
- 2 cups minced candied fruits, such as cherries, pineapple, orange, or a combination of one or more of these
- 1 cup finely chopped almonds, toasted

THE PREPARATION

To give Spumoni the attention it deserves, serve it in a sherbet glass or in a footed dessert cup.

To make it, soften the ice cream and fold in the candied fruits. Refreeze and, when ready to serve, spoon the ice cream first into the glass, then add a helping of sweetened whipped cream, and top this with a sprinkle of almonds. This delightful dessert can be served as a party refreshment with great success.

MEXICO

The many wonderful and lasting food ideas which have come to us from Mexico are too numerous to mention. Mexico's foods, eating habits, social and cultural life have had a great and lasting influence on all of the United States, but especially the South and Southwest.

Mexico's contributions to our cooking heritage which are best known and most frequently used are the bold seasonings which are many and varied. Among these are the chilis, comino, garlic, coriander, and oregano. Corn, chilis, and beans are among the most basic of the Mexican foods, and all of these have endless possibilities in methods of cooking and serving. Another food which Mexico claims credit for giving us is cocoa—chocolate, that comes from the cacao tree, which is native to southeast Mexico and an ingredient which Mexican cooks have a special talent in using. The list of tropical fruits found there that are served the year around would take a full chapter to write about.

A Church Supper Featuring Mexican Foods

Chicken Tortilla Casserole   Mexican Spoon Bread
Lettuce Salad
Fresh Papayas and Fresh Strawberries
Lime Juice
Coffee

The recipes required for this menu can be found in PART III of this book.

SPAIN

Because of its fascinating and turbulent history, Spain has one of the most interesting and exciting cuisines to be found in Europe. The Greek, Roman, and Moorish invaders left their mark on Spain's food history until this day. And in turn the Spaniards with their conquest into the southern part of the United States and in South America and Mexico have made their mark on our foods. The Creole dishes in the south of the United States are an evidence of this history.

Some of the most important seasonings in Spain are olive oil, peppers, garlic, saffron, and all kinds of herbs. They use combinations of these herbs to create foods with a culinary tradition which has made an impact throughout Europe.

Their famous paella is a national dish, similar to our Creole dishes, and is made of a blend of meat, poultry, fish and shellfish, combined with seasonings and served over rice. It is often seasoned with saffron.

For desserts the Spanish lean heavily on sweets made with honey or on chocolate, which they took from the Aztec Indians. Cocoa is said to have reached Spain in the 16th century, almost 200 years before tea and coffee were introduced to Europe.

A Church Supper Featuring Spanish Foods

Green Pepper Steaks   Spanish Rice
Shrimp Salad
Hard Rolls   Chocolate Cream Sauce
Wine
Coffee

The recipes required for this menu can be found in PART III of this book.

SWEDEN

Swedish food history has won fame around the world primarily through the *smorgasbord,* although American interpretations of what a smorgasbord is and how it is served seldom resemble the genuine, native smorgasbord. The word *smorgasbord* literally means *bread and butter table.* It had its origin long ago in rural areas in Sweden as a potluck supper or party, where each guest or family brought breads, butter, and something to go between two slices of bread, as their contribution to supplement whatever food the host had prepared. The smorgasbord is always served buffet style, but a buffet is *not* a smorgasbord, unless the menu consists of at least some of the traditional foods that brought the smorgasbord into existence. Americans have somehow got the idea that a buffet supper is a smorgasbord just because it is served buffet style. To serve a sumptuous and elegant smorgasbord for a church supper would be expensive and impractical. The elegant form consists of a whole range of fish dishes, potatoes, shellfish, smoked and pickled herring, roast beef, meat balls, vegetables, breads of many varieties, sweet cream butter, and an assortment of fruits and desserts. A smorgasbord requires from three to four fresh plates. The guest would need one plate for the relishes and salads, another for the fish dishes, still another for the heavy part of the meal, and a dessert bowl or small plate for the desserts.

Scandinavian homes have trimmed their smorgasbord down to a diminutive size, including now the ever-present herring, either pickled or smoked, or both, cheeses, dark breads, and always sweet cream butter. Obviously, Sweden and the other Scandinavian countries have a multitude of meals other than the smorgasbord. I am giving a menu for it here in some detail only because it has become so famous in every part of the world.

A Church Supper Featuring a Swedish Smorgasbord

Breads:
  Dark Rye, Whole Wheat
  Pumpernickel, French
  Hard Rolls
Sweet Cream Butter

Relish platters of:
  Cheeses, Pickles, Cold Cuts, Olives, Sweet Pickled Fruits, Fresh Cucumbers, Tomatoes, and Lettuce

Platters of: Pickled Herring,
  Smoked Herring,
  Marinated Shrimp in Wine Sauce

Hot Potato Salad
Swedish Meat Balls

Sweet-and-Sour Red Cabbage

Sour Cream Cookies

Fruit Compote

Wine
Coffee

SWEDISH MEAT BALLS

To make 10 generous servings

YOU WILL NEED

1/2 cup butter
1/2 cup finely chopped onions
1 cup fine bread crumbs made from French bread
1/3 cup water
1 cup sour cream
2 pounds ground beef, round preferred
1 pound ground pork
1 pound ground veal
3 eggs
2 teaspoons salt
1/2 teaspoon black pepper

THE PREPARATION

The secret of making real Swedish meat balls lies in the manner in which they are prepared. They should be quite small, formed separately, and cooked to remain separated. Sauté the onions in the butter until golden brown. Soak the bread crumbs for a few minutes in the water and sour cream. Combine the meats and sprinkle with salt and pepper. Add the eggs and bread crumbs and mix well. Drain the onions and add with all ingredients to the meats. Form into small balls, using two teaspoons to keep them small and uniform. Roll them in the palm of the hand to shape. They should be a little over 1 inch in diameter when shaped. Dip the spoons in cold water often while forming.

In a skillet with a handle fry the meat balls in what butter is left from sautéing the onions, add a little more butter if needed, and shake the pan continuously while the balls are frying to keep them shaped and to insure even cooking.

Fry a few at a time, and remove from the skillet when they are brown. Before adding more, strain out the scattered crumbs which will burn and keep the other balls from frying in good order. Continue frying until all are brown and cooked. When finished, add some milk or cream to the liquid and make a thin gravy. Pour this liquid over the meat balls and keep hot until time to serve. Delicious!

INDEX

INDEX

Angel Chocolate Pie, 192
Appetizers, 41
  Carrot Curls, 41
  Cheese Spreads, 41
  Dips and assorted appetizers, 41
  Fresh Fruits and Melon, 41
Apple Cake, Danish, 232
Apple Cake, Raw, 203
Apple Pie, Dutch, 194
Apple salads, 107
Appliances, 17
Apricot Cobbler, 197
Apricot Punch, 50

Baked Beans, 171
Baked Tomatoes, 181
Baker's Frosting, 209
Baking and roasting temperatures, 29
Barbecue Sauce, 132
Bean Roll, Fried, 171
Bechamel Sauce, 128
Beef
  All-Purpose Stew, 147
  amounts prepared for fifty, 25
  amounts to purchase, 21
  Brisket in Wine, 141
  Chili Con Carne, 148
  Chopped Sirloin Steaks, 142
  Green-Pepper Steaks, 143
  individual servings, 26
  Lasagne, Old-Style, 150
  Meat Balls and Spaghetti, 144
  Meat Loaf, 145
  Meat Loaf with Sour Cream Topping, 146
  Meat Pies, 148
  methods of cooking, 140
  Pot Roast, 146
  Spanish Meat Balls, 145
  Stroganoff with Noodles, 143
  Swedish Meat Balls, 244
Beef Cubes and Cabbage, 221
Beef Pot Roast, 146
Beef Stroganoff with Noodles, 143
Biscuits
  Bacon, 78
  Baking Powder, 76
  Buttermilk, 78
  Cheese, 77
  Mexican Chili, 78
  Sage, 77
  Sausage, 77
  Whole Wheat, 77
Bread
  Basic White, 55
  Dill and Onion, 65
  directions for freezing, 67
  French, 58
  Onion and Cottage Cheese, 63
  Pumpernickel, 61
  Raisin, 66
  Rye, 59
  suggestions for shapes and sizes, 68
  Whole Wheat, 57

Bread Stuffing for Turkey, 165
Breaded Pork Chops, 157
Breads and Bakery Products
  amounts to prepare, 24
  amounts to purchase, 21
  amounts to serve, 25
Breads, Sweet
  Applesauce Nut, 83
  Banana Nut, 83
  Carrot, 85
  Nut, 82
  Orange-Raisin, 84
Brisket in Wine, 141
Broccoli and Rice Casserole, 220
Broiling Chicken, 158
Brown Sauce, 127
Butter and Margarine
  amounts to purchase, 21
Butter Fluffs, 70
Buttermilk Pie, Old-Fashioned, 195

Cabbage au Gratin, 173
Cabbage, Creamed, 172
Cabbage Roll, Hungarian, 237
Cabbage Salad with Apples and Raisins, 111
Cabbage Salad with Carrots and Green Peppers, 111
Cabbage Salad with Pineapple, 111
Cakes
  amounts prepared, 24
  amounts to purchase, 21
  Carrot, 203
  Chocolate Fudge, 202
  Danish Apple, 232
  German Streusel, 235
  German's Sweet Chocolate, 201
  individual servings, 26
  Norwegian Coffee, 75
  Plain, 198
  Raw Apple, 203
  Sponge, all-purpose, 200
  White, 199
Carrot and Raisin Salad, 108
Carrot Bread, 85

Carrot Cake, 203
Carrots, Buttered, 175
Carrots with Orange Sauce, 175
Casseroles
  amounts prepared for fifty, 24
  Beef Cubes and Cabbage, 221
  Broccoli and Rice, 220
  Chicken and Tortillas, 221
  Chicken with Yellow Squash, 222
  Corn and Tomato, 223
  Crab and Shrimp, 223
  Ham and Red Beans with Fritos, 225
  individual servings, 26
  Spinach and Turkey, 226
  Tuna and Noodles, 225
Cereals and Cereal Products
  amounts prepared for fifty, 24
  amounts to purchase, 21
  individual servings, 26
Cheese, amounts to purchase, 21
Cheese Balls, 89
Cheese Biscuits, 77
Cheese Pastry, 188
Cheese Sauce, 127
Cheese Wafers, 89
Cheese Whole Wheat Rolls, 64
Cherry Cobbler, 196
Chicken
  amounts prepared for fifty, 25
  amounts to purchase, 22
  and Noodles, 162
  Breasts, Oriental, 163
  Creamed, 161
  Curried, 162
  Fricassee, 159
  hints for preparing and cooking chicken and fowl, 158
  with Pineapple, 164
Chicken and Tortilla Casserole, 221
Chicken with Yellow Squash Casserole, 222
Chicken Consommé Mold, 117
Chicken Salad, 114
  with Almonds and Cherries, 115

Chicken-Salad Sandwiches, 138
Chili Beans with Meat, 171
Chili Con Carne, 148
Chili-Tomato Sauce, 131
Chocolate Coffee, 46
Chocolate Cream Filling, 211
Chocolate Fudge Cake, 202
Chocolate Fudge Frosting, 210
Chocolate, Hot, 47
Chocolate Pie, 192
Cloverleaf Rolls, 69
Cobbler Crusts, 191
Cobblers
  Apricot, 197
  Cherry, 196
  suggestions for other fruit cobblers, 197
Cocoa Frosting, 209
Cocoa, Hot, 48
Cocktail Sauce, 132
Coconut Crust, 189
Coconut Custard, 214
Coffee
  amounts prepared for fifty, 24
  amounts to purchase, 21
  Café au Lait, 44
  Chocolate, 46
  Drip, 43
  Iced, 45
  individual servings, 25
  Percolated, 43
  Picnic-style, 44
  Steeped, 42
Coffee Cake, Norwegian, 75
Coffee Punch, 53
Cole Slaw, 110
Congealed Desserts
  Lime Mold with Angel Food Cake, 207
  Prune Whip Mold, 207
Congealed Salads
  Chicken Consommé Mold, 117
  Fruits with Fruit Juice, 119
  Pear and Cheese Mold, 118
Convenience Foods, 30
Cooked Salad Dressing, 124
  with Fruit Juices, 125
  with Sour Cream, 125
Cookies
  amounts prepared for fifty, 24
  Danish Sour Cream, 204
Cooking Talent, Search for, 15
Corn and Chicken Chowder, 97
Corn and Tomato Casserole, 223
Corn Breads
  Buttermilk, 80
  Spoon Bread, Deep South, 80
  Spoon Bread, Mexican-Style, 81
Corn Meal
  amounts prepared for fifty, 24
  amounts to purchase, 21
  individual servings, 26
Corn Pudding, 174
Corn Soup, Cream of, 92
Cornbread Stuffing for Turkey, 165
Cottage Cheese
  amounts to purchase, 21
Crab and Shrimp Casserole, 224
Cream Filling, 211
Cream Puffs, 88
Cream, Whipping and Coffee
  amounts to purchase, 21
Cream-Cheese Frosting, 209
Creamed Cabbage, 172
Creamed Chicken, 161
Creole Doughnuts (Beignets), 85
Crescent Rolls, 69
Curried Rice, 184
Custards
  Chocolate, 214
  Coconut, 214
  Orange, 214
  Vanilla, Basic Recipe, 213

Dairy Products
  amounts to purchase, 21
Danish Apple Cake, 232
Danish Open Sandwiches, 232
Danish Sour Cream Cookies, 204
Deep-Fat Frying, Chicken and Fowl, 159
Dill and Onion Bread, 65

Doughnuts, Creole, 85
Dutch Apple Pie, 194

Egg Sauce, 127
Eggplant, Baked, 179
English Triffle, 205
Equipment, 17
Equivalents and Measures, 18

Fillings and Sweet Sauces, 211
   Chocolate Cream Filling, 211
   Cream Filling, 211
   Lemon Filling or Sauce, 212
   Mocha Cream Filling, 211
   Pastry Cream Filling, 211
   Strawberry Cream Cheese Sauce, 215
Fillings for Sweet Rolls, 74
Fish
   amounts to purchase, 22
   cooking and purchasing shellfish, 166
Fish Fillets, Baked, 166
Freezing Breads, Directions for, 67
French Bread, 58
French Dressing, Basic Recipe, 121
   with chili sauce, 122
   with fruit juices, 121
   with poppy, celery, or sesame seed, 122
French Onion Soup, 96
Fricassee of Chicken, 159
Fried Bean Roll, 171
Frostings and Icings
   Baker's, 209
   Chocolate Fudge, 210
   Cocoa, 209
   Cream-cheese, 209
   Mocha Butter Cream, 209
   White Chocolate, 209
Frozen Fruit Salad, 105
Fruit Cobblers, 196-197
Fruit Punch, 49
Fruit Salad Dressing, 125
   with cooked dressing, 125

Fruit Salads
   amounts prepared for fifty, 25
   individual servings, 26
Fruits, Canned
   amounts to purchase, 21

Garnishes, 99
   Cheese Ball, 100
   Eggs, 100
   Fruits, 100
   Miscellaneous, 101
   Vegetables, 101
Gelatin Salads
   amounts prepared for fifty, 25
   individual servings, 26
German's Sweet Chocolate Cake, 201
Graham Cracker Crust, 188
Grape Punch, 50
Green Pepper Steaks, 143
Green Salad, Tossed, 108
   with carrots, 109
   with radishes, 109
   with red cabbage, 109
Grits
   amounts prepared for fifty, 24
   amounts to purchase, 21
   individual servings, 26
   Soufflé, 183

Ham
   Baked with Fruit Glaze, 153
   Baked with Orange Glaze, 153
   Creamed, 155
   Curried, 155
   Loaf, Congealed, 154
   Sandwiches, 137
   Sweet Sandwiches, 137
Ham and Red Bean Casserole, 225
Hamburgers for Fifty, 136
   trimmings for fifty, 137
Herbs and Spices, 27-29
Hot Chocolate, 47
Hot Cocoa, 48
Hot Potato Salad, 113

How to Cook Macaroni, Spaghetti and Noodles, 181
   amounts to cook and serve fifty, 181
Hungarian Cabbage Roll, 237

Icings for Cakes, 209

Kitchen Records, 13
   forms for record keeping, 14

Lamb
   amounts to purchase, 22
   amounts to serve, 158
   directions for cooking, 158
   Ribs and Chops, 158
   Roast Leg of Lamb, 158
Lasagne, Old-Style, 150
Leavening Agents
   amounts to use, 29
Leftover Turkey, 165
Leftovers, a Soup, 96
Lemon Chess Pie, 193
Lemon Filling or Sauce, 212
Lime Mold with Angel Food Cake, 207
Lime-Sherbet Punch, 52

Macaroni
   amounts prepared for fifty, 24
   amounts to purchase, 21
   individual servings, 26
Macaroni and Cheese, 182
Mayonnaise, Basic Recipe, 122
   with blue cheese, 123
   with cucumbers, 123
Measures and Equivalents, 18
Meat
   amounts prepared for fifty, 25
   amounts to purchase, 22
   individual servings, 26
   methods of cooking, 140
Meat Balls and Spaghetti, 144
Meat Balls, Swedish, 244

Meat Loaf, 145
Meat Loaf Potluck Supper for Fifty, 37
Meat Loaf with Sour Cream, 146
Meat Pie, 148
Meat Salads
   amounts prepared for fifty, 25
Menus
   A Danish Supper, 232
   A French Supper, 234
   A German Supper, 235
   A Hungarian Supper, 237
   An Italian Supper, 239
   A Mexican Supper, 241
   A Spanish Supper, 242
   A Swedish Supper, 243
Meringue Shells, Individual, 190
Meringue Shell for Pie, 190
Metric Conversion Factors, 19
Milk, amounts to purchase, 21
Mint-Butter Sauce, 130
Mocha Butter Cream, 209
Mocha Cream Filling, 211
Mornay Sauce, 129
Muffins
   Orange Marmalade, 79
   Pecan, 79
   Plain, 78
   Raisin, 79
Mushroom Sauce, 126

Noodles
   amounts prepared for fifty, 24
   amounts to purchase, 21
   how to cook, 181
   individual servings, 26
Norwegian Coffee Cake, 75
Nut Bread, Basic, 82
   Applesauce Nut, 83
   Banana Nut, 83

Onion & Cottage Cheese Bread, 63
Orange-Cider Punch, 51
Orange Custard, 214
Orange-Raisin Bread, 84

Pan Rolls, 68
Panfrying Chicken and Fowl, 158
Parker House Rolls, 69
Parsley-Butter Sauce, 129
Pastry Cream Filling, 211
Pear and Cheese Mold, 118
  with grapes, 119
Pie
  Angel Chocolate, 192
  Chocolate, 192
  Dutch Apple, 194
  Lemon Chess, 193
  Old-Fashioned Buttermilk, 195
  Pumpkin, 195
Pie Crusts
  Cobbler, 191
  Coconut, 189
  Cheese Pastry, 188
  for eight 8-inch pies, 187
  Graham Cracker Crumb, 188
  Meringue shell for one pie, 190
  Meringue shells, 190
  Vanilla Wafer, 188
Pizza, 86
  spreads for pizzas, 87
Plain Cake, Basic Recipe, 198
Pork
  amounts to purchase, 22
  Baked Ham with Fruit Glaze, 153
  Baked Ham with Orange Glaze, 153
  Breaded Pork Chops, 157
  Creamed Ham, 155
  Curried Ham, 155
  Ham Loaf, 154
  methods for cooking, 152
  Pork Chops with Pineapple Slices, 157
Potato Salad, 112
Potato Soup, Cream of, 91
Potatoes au Gratin, 176
Potatoes, Mashed, 175
Potluck Suppers
  an authentic potluck, 35
  supplemented potluck, 37
  the planned potluck, 36

Prepared Foods for Fifty, 24-25
  average individual servings, 25-26
Prune Whip Mold, 207
Puddings
  Corn, 174
  English Trifle, 205
  Sweet Roll, 206
Pumpernickel, 61
Pumpkin Pie, 195
Punch
  Apricot, 50
  Coffee, 53
  Fruit, basic, 49
  Grape, 50
  Hot Spiced Tea, 52
  Hot Spiced Tomato Juice, 54
  Lime-Sherbet, 52
  Orange-Cider, 51
  Raspberry, 50
  Witch's, 51
Purchasing Food for Fifty, 21

Raisin and Nut Stuffing for Turkey, 165
Raisin Bread, 66
Ranch-Style Beans, 171
Raspberry Punch, 50
Raw Apple Cake, 203
Red Bean Soup, 94
  Mexican, 95
Red Beans, 170
Relishes and Garnishes, 99
Reuben Sandwich, 138
Rice
  amounts prepared for fifty, 24
  amounts to purchase, 21
  basic recipe, 183
  individual servings, 26
  Spanish, 184
Roast Leg of Lamb, 158
Roasting and Baking Chicken, 159
Rolls
  Butter Fluffs and Fan Tans, 70
  Cheese Whole Wheat, 64
  Cloverleafs, 69
  Crescents, 69
  Fillings for sweet rolls, 74

Pan, 68
Parker House, 69
shapes and sizes, 68
Sweet Yeast, 72
Whole Wheat, 71
Yeast Bread, 70
Rye Bread, 59

Salad Dressings
  Blue Cheese Mayonnaise, 123
  Cooked dressing, basic, 124
  Cooked dressing with fruit juices, 125
  Cooked dressing with sour cream, 125
  Dressings for canned or fresh fruits, 104
  Dressings for vegetable-fruit combinations, 106
  French Dressing, basic, 121
  French Dressing with Chili Sauce, 122
  French Dressing with Fruit Juices, 121
  French Dressing with Poppy, Celery, or Sesame Seed, 122
  Mayonnaise Dressing, basic, 122
  Mayonnaise with Cucumbers, 123
  Thousand Island, 124

Salads
  amounts prepared for fifty, 25
  amounts to serve, 102
  Apple combinations, 107
  Apricots with Grapefruit Sections, 105
  Carrot and Pineapple, 108
  Carrot and Raisin, 108
  Chicken, 114
  Frozen Fruit, 105
    with Oranges, 106
  Fruit salad with canned fruits, 104
  Honeydew Melon with Strawberries, 103
  Hot Potato, 113
  individual servings, 26
  Melon-Melon, 103
  Papaya and Avocado, 103
  Pears with Orange Marmalade, 104
  Pears with Queen Ann Cherries, 105
  Potato, 112
  Shrimp, 115
  Strawberry and Avocado, 103
  Sweet Potato, 114
  Tossed Green, 108
  Tuna, 116
  Waldorf, 107

Salads, Congealed
  amounts to make and serve, 117
  Chicken Consommé Mold, 117
  Directions for gelatin combinations, 117
  Fruits with Fruit Juice, 119
  Pear and Cheese Mold, 118

Salmon Loaf, 168

Sandwiches
  Chicken Salad, 138
  Danish Open, 232
  Fillings for sandwiches, 135
  Grilled Cheese, 136
  Ham, 137
  Pimiento Cheese, 136
  preparing sandwiches ahead, 134
  Reùben, 138
  Sweet Ham, 137
  Tuna Salad, 137

Sauces for Meats and Vegetables
  Barbecue, 132
  Bechamel, 128
  Brown, 127
  Cheese, 127
  Chili-Tomato, 131
  Cocktail, 132
  Egg, 127
  Hot Mustard, 130
  Mint-Butter, 130
  Mornay, 129
  Mushroom, 126
  Parsley-Butter, 129
  Sweet Brown, 128
  Tomato, 131
  White, basic, 126
  Vegetable Stock, 130

253

Sausage Biscuits, 77
Sausage Stuffing for Turkey, 165
Seasonings
  for quantity foods, 27
  herbs and spices, 27
Shrimp Salad, 115
  with Potatoes, 116
Sirloin Steaks, Chopped, 142
Soups
  amounts for serving, 91
  amounts prepared for fifty, 25
  Corn and Chicken Chowder, 97
  Corn, Cream of, 92
  French Onion, 96
  individual servings, 26
  Leftovers, 96
  Mexican Bean, 95
  Potato, 91
  Red Bean, 94
  Split-Pea, 95
  Tomato, 93
Spaghetti
  amounts prepared for fifty, 24
  amounts to purchase, 21
  individual servings, 26
Spanish Meat Balls, 145
Spanish Rice, 184
Spiced Tea, Hot, 52
Spices and Herbs, 27
Spinach and Turkey Casserole, 226
Split-Pea Soup, 95
Sponge Cake, All-Purpose, 200
Spoon Bread, Deep South, 80
Spoon Bread, Mexican-Style, 81
Spreads for Pizzas, 87
Spumoni, 239
Squash, Yellow, 177
Stew, All-Purpose, 147
Stewed Tomatoes, Old-Style, 180
Stewing and Simmering Chicken and Fowl, 159
Strawberry Cream Cheese Sauce, 215
Streusel Cake, German, 235
Stuffings for Turkey
  Corn-Bread, 165
  Plain Bread, 165
  Raisin and Nut, 165
  Sausage, 165
Swedish Meat Balls, 244
Sweet and Sour Red Cabbage, 173
Sweet Brown Sauce, 128
Sweet Potato Puffs, 176
Sweet Potato Salad, 114
Sweet Roll Pudding, 206
Sweet Sauces and Fillings, 211
  see Fillings and Sweet Sauces
Sweet Yeast Breads and Rolls, 72

Tea
  amounts prepared for fifty, 24
  amounts to purchase, 21
  Hot, 46
  Hot Spiced, 52
  Iced, 47
  individual servings, 25
Thickening Agents
  amounts to use, 29
Thousand Island Dressing, 124
Tomato Juice, Hot Spiced, 54
Tomato Sauce, 131
Tomato Soup, Cream of, 93
Tuna and Noodles Casserole, 225
Tuna, Baked, 167
Tuna Salad, 116
  with Apples, 116
Tuna Sandwiches, 137
Turkey
  amounts prepared for fifty, 25
  amounts to purchase, 22
  individual servings, 26
  Roast, 164
  Stuffings for turkey, 165
  Tetrazzini, 161
  Turkey and Spinach Casserole, 226
  Turkey leftovers, 165

Utensils, 17

Vanilla Custard, Basic Recipe, 213

Veal
  amounts to purchase, 22
Vegetable Salads
  amounts prepared for fifty, 25
  Cabbage, Carrots, and Green Peppers, 111
  Cabbage-Pineapple, 111
  Cabbage with Apples and Raisins, 111
  Cole Slaw, 110
  Hot Potato, 113
  individual servings, 26
  Mixed Vegetables, 110
  Potato, 112
  Sweet Potato, 114
  Tossed Green, 108
Vegetable Stock Sauce, 130
Vegetables
  amounts prepared for fifty, 25
  amounts to purchase, 22
  Baked Beans, 171
  Baked Tomatoes, 181
  Buttered Carrots, 175
  Cabbage au gratin, 173
  canned, 170
  Carrots with Orange Sauce, 175
  cooking guide for vegetables, 169
  Corn Pudding, 174
  creamed, 170
  Creamed Cabbage, 172
  Dried Beans, 170
  Eggplant, Baked, 179
  Fried-Bean Roll, 171
  frozen, 170
  individual servings, 26
  Mashed Potatoes, 175
  Potatoes au gratin, 176
  Ranch-style Beans, 171
  Stewed Tomatoes, Old-style, 180
  Sweet and Sour Red Cabbage, 173
  Sweet Potato Puffs, 176
  Yellow Squash, 177
    Mexican Style, 178
  Zucchini Parmesan, 178
  Zucchini with Tomatoes and Onions, 179

Waldorf Salad, 107
  with Carrots and Raisins, 107
  with Oranges and Grapes, 107
White Cake, 199
White Chocolate Frosting, 209
White Sauce, 126
Whole Wheat Biscuits, 77
Whole Wheat Bread, 57
Whole Wheat Rolls, 71
Wieners, Barbecued, 152
Wieners, Sweet and Sour, 151
Wieners with Sauerkraut, 152
Witch's Punch, 51

Yeast Bread Rolls, 68
Yellow Squash, 177
  Mexican Style, 178

Zucchini Parmesan, 178
Zucchini with Tomatoes and Onions, 179

255